T0115037

Is God Evil?

MIRNA HANNA Ph.D.

BALBOA.
PRESS

A DIVISION OF HAY HOUSE

Balboa Press books may be ordered through booksellers or by contacting:

Balboa Press
A Division of Hay House
1663 Liberty Drive
Bloomington, IN 47403
www.balboapress.com
1 (877) 407-4847

Because of the dynamic nature of the Internet, any web addresses or links contained in this book may have changed since publication and may no longer be valid. The views expressed in this work are solely those of the author and do not necessarily reflect the views of the publisher, and the publisher hereby disclaims any responsibility for them.

The author of this book does not dispense medical advice or prescribe the use of any technique as a form of treatment for physical, emotional, or medical problems without the advice of a physician, either directly or indirectly. The intent of the author is only to offer information of a general nature to help you in your quest for emotional and spiritual well-being. In the event you use any of the information in this book for yourself, which is your constitutional right, the author and the publisher assume no responsibility for your actions.

Any people depicted in stock imagery provided by Thinkstock are models, and such images are being used for illustrative purposes only. Certain stock imagery © Thinkstock.

Printed in the United States of America.

ISBN: 978-1-4525-9337-1 (sc)
ISBN: 978-1-4525-9339-5 (hc)
ISBN: 978-1-4525-9338-8 (e)

Library of Congress Control Number: 2014903961

Balboa Press rev. date: 05/05/2014

Part I.   Who is God? The Mechanics of Consciousness

Part II.   The Energetic Harness: Reality as a Prison

Part III. The Hidden Science of Cocreation

Part IV. Back to Godhood in a Few Steps

Human beings sit in a cave, in chains, their backs to the entrance. The shadows of things moving outside are projected by the light onto an inner wall of the cave. As the prisoners have never been outside the cave since birth, they believe these shadows are reality. One of them succeeds in freeing himself and walks outside into the light. He realizes that he has lived his whole life in the shadow of an illusion. Delighted by his discovery, he returns to the cave to communicate it to the others. Violence erupts between the one who ventured outside and those who do not want to understand. The story ends with the death of the person that had gained insight into reality.

The Allegory of the Cave
Plato (Wikipedia)

Most of us are familiar with Plato's allegory of the cave where people only get to see shadows that they mistake for reality. What if we were those cavemen?

We are born and schooled; we find a job; we get married and have children; we age and die. We are told that this is the only formula for happiness, and that it was intended by God, who created us in his image. This is all we know. If this is perfect, how come we suffer?

The premise is that we are clueless despite our God-given values and scientific breakthroughs. If we came to know all the things that we are currently unaware of, we would do almost everything differently, and what we are unaware of is the hidden part of the iceberg. The first clue that allows us to put the pieces of the puzzle together is that matter is energy, and energy obeys the laws of science as demonstrated through the lens of quantum physics. Energy is consciousness, which means that what we don't see with our physical eyes and label as the spiritual realm, is not opposed to science, which is taking baby steps toward explaining its complex workings and mechanics.

The dichotomy that exists between spirituality and science in our present paradigm is extremely misleading. It is one of the many cognitive distortions that pervade the construct that we call "reality." What if most of what we think we know is not true?

What if the construct that we call reality comprises many of these distortions? What if these viruses were seeded on purpose? What if, while we think that we have free will, we are actually plugged into a matrix of cognitive distortions and programmed like robots to sleepwalk through life? If this is true, then who benefits from having the human race imprisoned in this energetic harness, building an entire reality system on deceitful illusions?

What if the array of limitations that we experience daily, like ailment, scarcity, aging, and even physical death, were not part of the plan? What if something went terribly wrong? What if the real conflict was not between good and evil, but rather between a universal truth and a universal lie that has kept us since the beginning of recorded history chained to the walls of the cave, with our backs turned to the light, building our entire belief system on mere shadows?

What if health, abundance, playfulness, the power to manifest, and eternal life were our divine rights?

Your time is limited, so don't waste it living someone else's life. Don't be trapped by dogma—which is living with the results of other people's thinking. Don't let the noise of others' opinions drown your own inner voice. And most important, have the courage to follow your heart and intuition. They somehow already know what you truly want to become. Everything else is secondary.

Steve Jobs

Part I

Who Is God?
The Mechanics of Consciousness

Chapter 1
The Nature of Matter

The Particle/Wave Duality and the Matter/Consciousness Dichotomy

First, let us explore the nature of matter. Some interesting leads have been uncovered on the subject in quantum physics, demonstrating that what appears to be solid matter is in reality made of two components: a handful of quanta and a majority of void. Quanta means energy, which is another word for consciousness. Investigating the nature of matter through the lens of quantum physics leads inevitably to talk about consciousness. Matter and consciousness are not only linked, matter is a manifestation of consciousness.

Our body and all solid matter are made of atoms. The structure of an atom consists of a nucleus located at the center, with electrons revolving around it. The distance between the nucleus and each electron is equivalent to a football field. Atoms are therefore made mainly of void with subatomic particles floating around; their numbers vary according to the nature of the atom.

What are subatomic particles made of? They are either elementary particles or composites of elementary particles, like the atom's nucleus. When studied, elementary particles, which are the smallest indivisible particles of solid matter discovered so far, have not only demonstrated wave properties—hence the particle/wave duality paradox—but they have also shown that their behavioral properties are not set in stone. They are "probabilities."

The wave/particle duality is the result of experiments conducted by quantum physicists studying the behavior of elementary particles. These series of experiments have shown that an elementary particle can behave either as a particle or as a wave. This paradox is best illustrated by what is referred to in quantum physics as the "double slit experiment." Two parallel screens are used, the first one comprising two identical vertical slits through which elementary particles are fired, targeting the second screen. When elementary particles are fired through one of the two vertical slits, they strike the second screen and form a pattern similar in size and shape to the slit through which they were fired. A similar result is obtained when particles are fired though the second slit, as they also hit the screen forming a vertical line. The logical sequence would be that when both slits are simultaneously opened, the pattern formed on the second screen by the particles would be that of two vertical lines (Figure 1). The result of the experiment was baffling because several lines appeared on the screen, despite the presence of only two slits (Figure 1). This would usually occur only in the case of waves, as a result of the interference pattern between them (Figure 2).

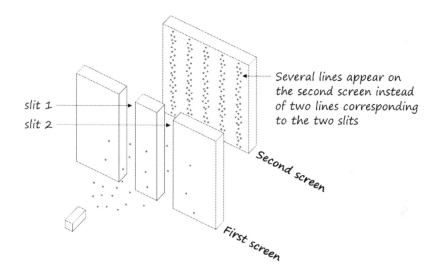

Figure 1. The double slit experiment: Instead of forming two straight lines, particles behave like waves, forming several lines on the second screen.

This experiment demonstrates the dual nature of matter and also raises questions about the nature of reality itself. What is more real: the particle or the wave nature of the elementary particles that form matter? Even when carried out with a single electron, the double slit experiment still exhibits patterns of interference (Figure 2). How can one single electron interfere with itself? This would mean that one electron passed through both slits at the same time. How can this be true without defying the very nature of reality itself?

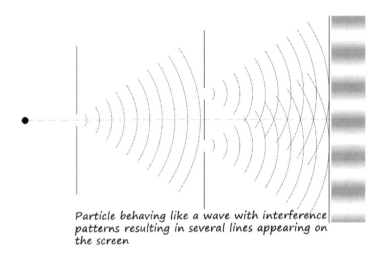

Particle behaving like a wave with interference patterns resulting in several lines appearing on the screen

Figure 2. Single particle behaving like a wave

More baffling results occurred when a monitoring device was introduced in order to observe through which slit the electron passed. As a result of the introduction of the observer, the electron behaved as a particle, and the interference pattern ceased. The outcome of the experiment was thus altered through "observation," i.e. consciousness. This implies that reality is a set of possibilities, and the one that comes into materialization is simply the one that we bring awareness to. Something exists when consciousness is brought to it; otherwise it is only a possibility. Consciousness shapes physical reality and beyond, as matter is only one of consciousness' multiple expressions.

Matter Is Consciousness

Consciousness is first down-stepped as sound and light before it manifests as matter. The series of experiments described previously demonstrate indirectly that 1) sound and light are the interface between consciousness and matter, which explains why particles behave like waves, and 2) consciousness shapes matter since nothing is real until it is observed.

Down stepping

Not only does consciousness precede matter, it also shapes it. Reality is not linear; it is a set of probabilities. The one that materializes is the one toward which consciousness is channeled: matter is a state of consciousness.

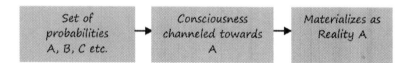

What we don't see precedes and shapes what we see according to precise mechanics. This "intangible software" forms the blueprint of physical reality.

Intangible Software that forms the
blueprint of physical reality

How real are we? We are a handful of quanta floating around in a three-dimensional void. This is the most exciting thing we can be told about ourselves because it means that we are a wide array of possibilities, and that our lives are always in the making. Every moment, we can choose to be the best of who we can become.

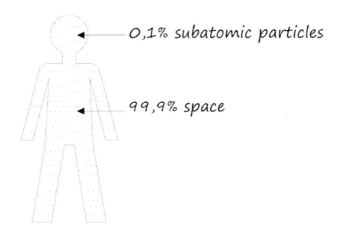

0,1% subatomic particles

99,9% space

"Energy is consciousness, and consciousness is energy."

E'Asha Ashayana

"Although you appear in earthly form, your essence is pure consciousness."

Rumi

Chapter 2
From Consciousness to Matter

Scalability and Fractality

Physical reality has a holographic nature. Its true substance is consciousness that projects itself onto a three-dimensional screen. Each person's script is a reflection of his or her own consciousness, or energy signature. In terms of sustainability, physical reality is barely real, whereas consciousness is— physicality is subject to entropy, but consciousness is eternal.

Consciousness manifests itself through a stepping-down process that consists of an expansion cycle during which creation individuates from Source. The expansion cycle is followed by a contraction cycle, wherein individuated consciousness returns back to Source. The stepping-down process is based on the two principles of scalability and fractality.

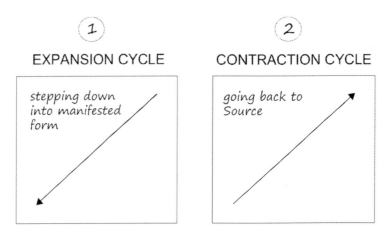

The manifested universe that is known to us, as well as the parts that we are unaware of, originate from a Source commonly called God. We can compare the process of manifestation from Source to an electrical circuit, with Source being the power plant that feeds millions of light bulbs. Source manifests itself into trillions of planets, embodied and disembodied conscious entities, though the stepping-down process, which is comparable to an electrical circuit in terms of scalability and fractality. Stepping down into manifested form is an expansion cycle, whereas going back to Source is a contraction cycle.

A first individuation from Source occurs with the formation of a wave of conscious entities that step down progressively into the lower dimensions, each time splicing into a larger number of individuated beings. Stepping down entails a progressive loss of energetic magnitude, which can be illustrated through the example of the power plant and the domestic light bulb. The energy generated by a power plant cannot directly feed a hundred-watt light bulb because the magnitude will cause the light bulb to explode. Therefore, it has to be scaled down through its transmission to a substation that feeds the distribution transformers, which then feed the domestic power outlets. At each level, there is a distribution and a scaling-down of power. The same applies to the higher soul that cannot embody because its high frequency does not match the density level of the physical plane. If the higher soul were to enter the physical plane, the human body would not be able to withstand such a quantum of energy. Therefore, it scales itself down, and only a small fraction that is equal to the quantum of energy that the human body can withstand embodies. This is referred to as the incarnated soul.

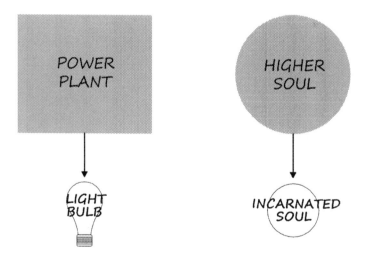

The stepping-down process is also based on the principle of fractality, since all the elements that originate from an identical source share the same components or essence, only on a reduced scale.

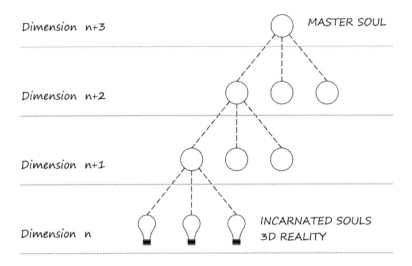

Dimension n+3   MASTER SOUL

Dimension n+2

Dimension n+1

Dimension n   INCARNATED SOULS
3D REALITY

The Stepping-Down Process

The stepping-down process, or expansion cycle, is when Source expands itself to form dimensions each characterized by different energetic and physical properties, including the nature of atoms. The closer a dimension is to Source, the higher its frequency and the lower its density. In the lower dimensions, atoms are carbon-based, which explains why matter is so dense.

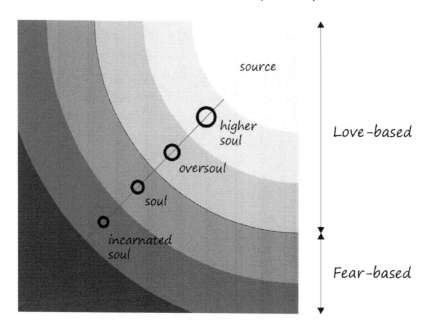

An incarnated soul in the three-dimensional world is stepped down from its higher soul stationed in higher dimensions, to which it remains connected through the "spiritual cord." The multidimensional structure of our spiritual anatomy implies that we exist simultaneously in different dimensions. Moving through dimensions is a process based on precise mechanics, where the energetic properties of an entity must match those of a specific dimension. For example, an entity burdened with fear-based consciousness, with the physical properties that such an energy entails, cannot ascend to higher, love-based dimensions. The widespread fear-based consciousness in the lower dimensions hinders the contraction cycle that is supposed to follow every expansion cycle, where an entity goes back to Source after having experienced individuation.

Cycles of Expansion and Contraction and the Divine Blueprint

The stepping down of consciousness takes place according to a "divine blueprint" characterized by precise mathematical and physical properties. During an expansion cycle, an individuated consciousness splices into several entities of smaller magnitude that manifest in the lower dimensions. This process does not take place randomly; it obeys precise mechanics. If, during the expansion cycle, an individuated entity starts miscreating and being misaligned with Source through fear-based behavior, the mathematical and physical properties of its divine blueprint become altered. This mutation hinders the contraction cycle because the original imprint for health of the divine blueprint is required in order for it to merge back with its counterparts in the higher dimensions.

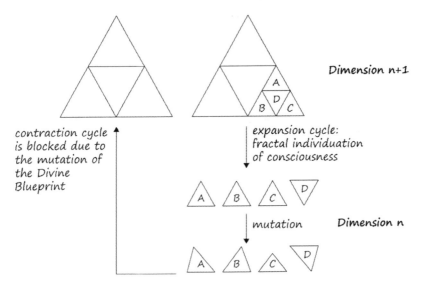

Figure 3. The role of the divine blueprint in the expansion and contraction cycles

Thousands of years of fear-based consciousness have altered the original mathematical and physical properties of our race's divine blueprint. The consequence is that the natural contraction cycle has been hindered, leaving individuated entities trapped in the lower dimensions, having to undergo endless cycles of reincarnation.

The Role of Sound and Light in Manifested Consciousness

Consciousness first translates as sound and light, the two primary fields that precede manifestation. Sound is the first field birthed from the unmanifested, hence "In the beginning was the Word." Sound travels through a medium, and therefore its speed depends on the physical properties of the medium through which it travels. Light travels through a vacuum, and therefore its speed is constant.

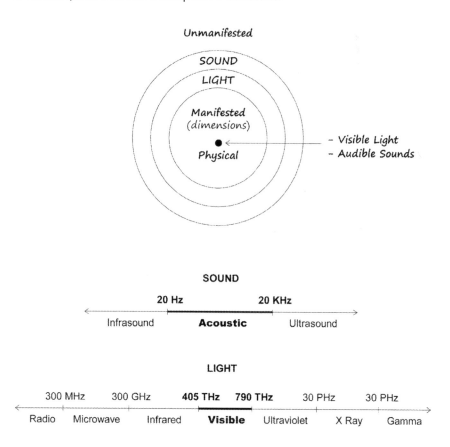

Manifestation is based upon the combination of patterns of sound and light following a certain template called a "divine blueprint." This template consists of a hierarchy of energy vortices each having a specific color, sound, and frequency. The system of relations that these energy vortices form with each other is based upon a precise, "sacred" geometric code.

Light and sound frequency patterns are not random; they have an impact on both our spiritual and biological anatomies. This explains why the frequency of angry words is detrimental and why people undergo light therapy to cure depressive moods. The frequency of audible sounds and visible images, which are patterns of light, is constantly affecting the imprint for health of our divine blueprint, thus determining our state of alignment with the matrix of creation.

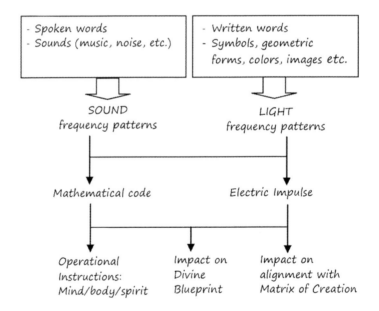

Fear-Based Consciousness and Inorganic Sound and Light

The two primary ingredients of the secret anatomy that underlies biological form are sound and light. Fear-based consciousness causes these two premanifestation elements to become inorganic and misaligned with the matrix of creation. The presence of inorganic sound and light is comparable to that of cancerous cells in a living organism. Because our earthly dimension is mainly fear-based, inorganic sound and light pervade all living organisms. Consequently, the divine blueprint of all earthly creatures, including the planet itself, is in a state of misalignment with the matrix of creation. This explains why our system is governed by the law of entropy.

Fear-based consciousness translates physically as inorganic sound and light that have a reversed frequency as compared to their organic counterparts. This inorganic presence causes mutations and disease on all levels of the intangible and biological anatomies, as well as a string of anomalies in the expansion and contraction cycles. The particularity of human consciousness, and other forms that are evolving in our system, is that they have four primary ingredients instead of two: organic sound and light and inorganic sound and light. Each of these four components has a different frequency, and since they are found in proportions that vary from one individual to the other, each person has a specific energy signature. If the inorganic component is found in higher proportions, then the energy signature is reversed as opposed to a healthy one.

The presence of inorganic light wreaks havoc with the spiritual and biological anatomies, including the deactivation of DNA and the degeneration of the physical body, since it alters the natural flows of energy with Source that translate as illness, aging, and ultimately physical death.

Chapter 3
The Secret Anatomy

Matrix of Creation and Accretion of Consciousness

Whenever an expansion cycle is taking place, units of consciousness populate the universe, forming a canvas referred to as the matrix of creation. They form a first layer similar to a grid, upon which they further accrete according to certain patterns, thus manifesting a diversity of forms.

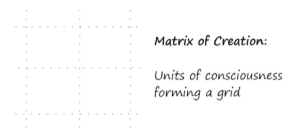

Matrix of Creation:

Units of consciousness forming a grid

The matrix of creation is the grid upon which units of consciousness accrete to create different forms, such as a human being, an animal, a plant, a pebble, etc. When it comes to earthly creatures, human beings represent the most sophisticated accretion pattern and therefore hold more consciousness than other living organisms, which gives them abilities like reasoning, planning, speech, and free will.

A human being may be a more sophisticated form of consciousness than a flower, but they are both made of the same essence, i.e. units of consciousness emanating from Source. The pattern according to which units of consciousness accrete is the divine blueprint.

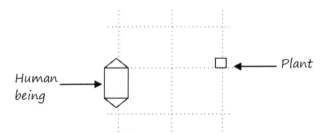

Figure 4. Accretion patterns of two different forms of consciousness on the matrix of creation

Mathematical and Physical Properties of Manifested Form: The Role of the Divine Blueprint

The blueprint of a house represents the interface between the concept, which is the intangible component, and the building, the tangible result. Similarly, the divine blueprint represents the interface between consciousness and manifested form, and is as sophisticated as the biological body. The divine blueprint codes the repartition of sound and light, the first fields to manifest from pure consciousness, along primary, secondary, tertiary, etc. energy vortices and lines.

Eggs, sugar, flour, and chocolate are the ingredients of a cake, combined according to a certain recipe. Sound and light are the ingredients of manifested form, with the divine blueprint acting as the recipe. It determines the color and sound frequency of each energy vortex and the repartition of the energy vortices along a geometric template. Other components of the divine blueprint are the non-biological DNA template and the merkaba vehicle.

Not only do units of consciousness accrete following a geometric template, but they are also characterized by physical properties, such as the cycle of fusion and fission of particles and the angular rotation of particle spin, which both determine the frequency level. Variations in frequency translate as different density levels from gross matter to unmanifested form, which explains how different dimensions can coexist at the same time while remaining undetected to one another. Even though different radio stations coexist, you can only listen to the one that matches the radio frequency you are tuned to. If the radio is tuned to 102 FM, it cannot catch a station broadcasting on 104 FM. Similarly, the universe comprises a multitude of dimensions with different frequency levels. Even physical reality occurs within bandwidths depending on a person's frequency level. A beggar on the streets of Bangladesh is evolving and having his physical experience in a different bandwidth than a Hollywood movie star.

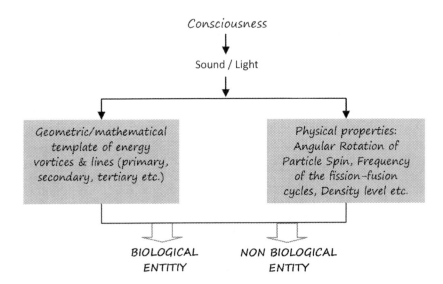

Each dimension is characterized by a divine blueprint—a cycle of fission-fusion, an angular rotation of particle spin, a frequency and density level, a specific nature of atoms, and a maximum capacity for the accretion of consciousness.

Mathematical/Geometric Template and Embodiment of Consciousness

Just like a house has a blueprint, a physical body has a skeleton, and a text has a topic and a structure, we humans and other forms of creation have a mathematical/geometric template that is one of the primary components of the divine blueprint. The word "divine" refers to the love-based code that is the language of Source; it is the original imprint for health prior to any distortions or mutations. Each energy vortex is associated with a color, a sound, and a frequency. The divine blueprint regulates the distribution of these ingredients to create the human recipe. An example of such a geometric template is the tree of life. The relation between the twelve spheres, or energy vortices, is based upon precise mathematical and geometric proportions. It is only one component of our sophisticated secret anatomy, which comprises several overlaid systems of energy vortices like the seven primary chakras.

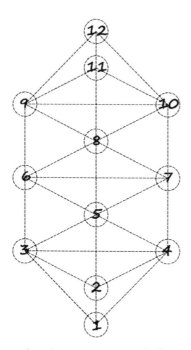

Figure 5. Geometric template known as "tree of life"
(Source: A'shayana & A'hzayana Deane)

The geometric template is the primary grid upon which consciousness accretes to create an individuated form on the matrix of creation. The twelve energy centers of the geometric template, to which twelve strands of the DNA template correspond, allow for the embodiment of twelve dimensions of consciousness. Fear-based consciousness and inorganic light block energy centers and lines in the geometric template and deactivate or disassemble DNA strands, which curtails the accretion of consciousness. The less consciousness the physical body holds, the less frequency it has and the denser it is, the more vulnerable it becomes to dysfunction, including disease and decay.

The Nonbiological DNA Template

There is more to DNA than meets the eye. The part that holds the genetic code for the human body represents less than 90 percent of the biological DNA, and science is still unable to elucidate the function of what is called "junk DNA." Besides the biological DNA, there is a nonbiological DNA template that is another important component of the divine blueprint. It comprises twelve strands of DNA that correspond to the twelve dimensions of consciousness that can be embodied by a human being. Most of these strands are deactivated, which explains the presence in the biological DNA of more than 90 percent junk that doesn't seem to hold any function in the human genome. Disabling the DNA causes major dysfunctions in the spiritual anatomy, namely a loss of natural abilities; extrasensory perception, multidimensional awareness, transdimensional travel, and biological longevity are built-in abilities that only function when the DNA is fully operational.

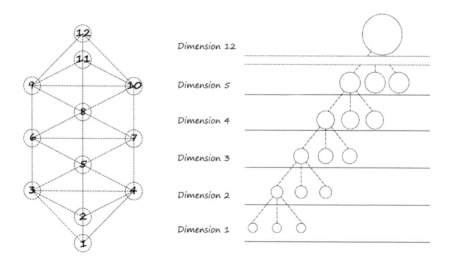

Merkaba Vehicle

The merkaba vehicle is the component of the divine blueprint that allows for transdimensional travel, also known as ascension. In order for the merkaba to function properly, the twelve strands of the original DNA template must be fully activated. When the nonbiological DNA template is restored, the biological junk DNA reassembles again and the merkaba becomes operational.

The merkaba vehicle is formed by two counter-rotating electrical and magnetic fields surrounding the body. It enables transdimensional travel, thus acting like a personal spaceship invisible to the naked eye. It is an ascension vehicle allowing for the body to translocate to a higher dimension at the end of its life cycle on Earth. Merkaba vehicles are currently dysfunctional because of the mutations in the divine blueprint and the blockages in DNA. They have been deactivated for eons, and contemporary humanity has no recollection of their existence; today transdimensional travel only qualifies as sci-fi material.

The most notable consequence of the dysfunction of the merkaba vehicle is physical death. Restoring the divine blueprint to its original settings causes a simultaneous healing of the merkaba vehicle, which is our birthright. All the components of the divine blueprint, including DNA, must be restored to their original settings in order for the merkaba vehicle to regain its proper functions.

Cycle of Fission-Fusion

Another property of the accretion of consciousness, besides mathematical templates, is the cycle of fission and fusion that allows "antematter particles" to form particles and antiparticles. Expansion takes place when the fission of antematter particles gives birth to particles and antiparticles. Contraction follows expansion through the fusion of particles and antiparticles that merge back together, returning to their original state of antematter. Through this process, consciousness cyclically manifests and demanifests itself.

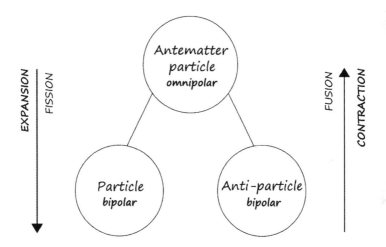

The faster the fission and fusion of particles, the shorter the cycle and the higher the frequency. Each dimension is characterized by a cycle of fission-fusion, which determines, along with the nature of the atoms, the frequency and density level of manifested forms of consciousness.

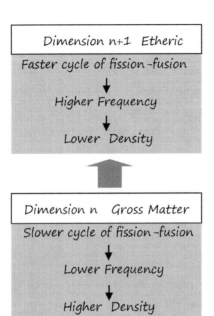

Angular Rotation of Particle Spin

Particles spin according to a certain angle, called the angular rotation of particle spin (ARPS). This difference in angular rotation is what allows for several dimensions to coexist simultaneously within the same space. A difference of 45° in ARPS translates as a transdimensional shift. Physical properties like the cycle of fission-fusion, ARPS, and the nature of the atoms are important attributes of all manifested forms of consciousness; they determine the frequency and density levels that dictate the dimension in which an individuated consciousness is evolving. Hence, there is a correlation between the cycle of fission-fusion, the nature of the atoms, ARPS, and the accretion of consciousness.

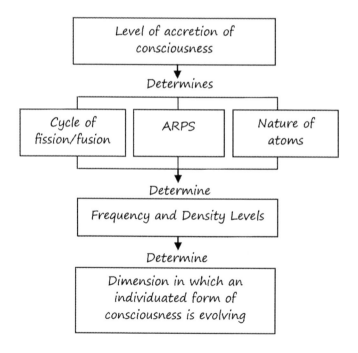

The Multi-Layered Secret Anatomy

Our complex secret anatomy is a proof that what we see—in this instance, biological form—is only the tip of the iceberg in relation to what exists. Its workings represent only a fraction of the complex mechanics of manifestation. Sound and light as the primary ingredients of manifested form are combined according to several overlaid templates in order to create the divine blueprint that codes biological form.

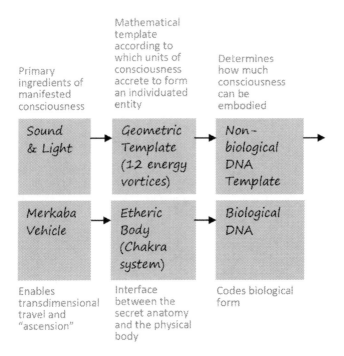

The overlaid components of our invisible anatomy are pervaded at all levels by inorganic elements. The contemporary human template has only a few operational strands of nonbiological DNA instead of twelve. This explains the loss of multidimensional awareness and why we traverse life in a state of amnesia, with the three-dimensional world and our short life span as the only horizon. The deactivation of DNA is also evidenced by the disruption of natural energy flows within the body, causing its decay.

Upgrading and Downgrading of Individuated Consciousness

Energy is always in motion. Two factors determine how an individuated consciousness will evolve: the accretion of consciousness and the presence of inorganic light. The accretion of consciousness is the factor that causes an individuated consciousness to upgrade, whereas the presence of inorganic light causes it to downgrade.

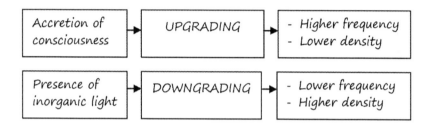

A flower represents a smaller accretion of consciousness than a human being. At the same time, it comprises a lower percentage of inorganic light because it doesn't have the free will to miscreate, which is a prerogative of more sophisticated forms of consciousness. Human consciousness has the choice to accrete consciousness by cocreating, or to reinforce inorganic light through miscreation.

Level of accretion of consciousness

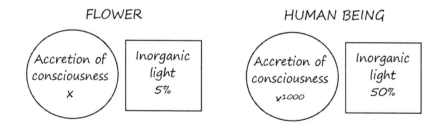

Chapter 4
The Intangible Software

Reality's Invisible Code

The findings of quantum physics question the common belief that matter is solid, and that reality is a universal truth rather than a construct. The nature of matter is consciousness that projects as reality. Consciousness is the fabric of manifested and unmanifested creation, shaping physical reality and beyond. Every form of consciousness has a specific code formed by patterns of sound and light that obey specific mathematical and physical properties. A flower and a human being are both manifested forms of consciousness with a different code, entailing a specific arrangement of sound and light patterns for each. We are not consciously aware of that code because it is intangible to the five senses. Through our conscious minds, we only have a limited cognition of the ubiquitous consciousness that forms the canvas upon which creation is interwoven. This intangible software can be apprehended primarily through the mental and emotional bodies. They are at the same time components of the secret anatomy and doorways to it, since the cognition of the intangible software is enabled by thoughts and emotions.

The secret anatomy as the intangible software comprises inorganic components like the subconscious mind and shadow-self, caused by the presence of fear-based consciousness.

The Conscious and Subconscious Minds and Their Relation to the Brain

Science acknowledges that the conscious mind is located in the brain, as this organ is the seat of reasoning, logic, abstract thinking, vision, planning, language, hand skills, etc. If the conscious mind corresponds to the human brain, then what about the subconscious mind? The subconscious mind is the seat of automatic reflexes, such as driving, as well as automatic reactions to environmental stimuli. The conscious mind represents less than one percent of the human mind, whereas the subconscious mind, which is not located in the brain, represents more than 99 percent.

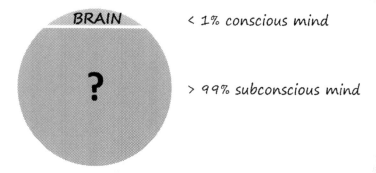

BRAIN   < 1% conscious mind

?   > 99% subconscious mind

What we refer to as the mind is far more sophisticated than we think. The brain/mind dichotomy stems from the recent discovery that, just like music is not in the instrument, the mind does not correspond entirely to a biological organ called the brain.

Brainwaves

The millions of cells that form the human brain use electricity to communicate with each other. This electrical activity forms five major types of brainwaves known as gamma, beta, alpha, theta, and delta.

- Gamma: intense cerebral activity
  > 40 pulses per second on the Hertz scale

- Beta: conscious awake state
  13–60 pulses per second on the Hertz scale

- Alpha: relaxation state with eyes closed
  7–13 pulses per second on the Hertz scale

- Theta: sleep state
  4–7 pulses per second on the Hertz scale

- Delta: deep sleep state
  0.1–4 pulses per second on the Hertz scale

The alpha and theta brainwaves represent the interface between the conscious and subconscious mind; it is only when the brain activity is slow that the subconscious can be accessed. The theta brainwave is the optimal doorway to the subconscious mind, as healing, manifestation, and access to past memories occur during this state.

Children operate mainly in the theta brainwave, unlike adults, who only experience this state during sleep, meditation, or deep relaxation. Because the doorway to the subconscious mind is permanently opened during early childhood, children act like psychic sponges and are deeply imprinted by environmental stimuli. Hence, the programming of the subconscious mind occurs mainly during early childhood. It is an inflicted program, since children have no control over their environment. This early involuntary programming forms the blueprint, or script, for future life events. Fortunately, the subconscious mind can be reprogrammed in order to reverse detrimental childhood programming.

The Seat of the Subconscious Mind

The primary function of the subconscious mind, besides automatic reflexes, is storing unprocessed fear-based consciousness like negative programs, mind viruses, toxic beliefs, and trauma. The part of the subconscious mind where unprocessed fear-based consciousness is stored will be referred to as the shadow-self. It gives birth to the negative ego, another inorganic component that causes further distortions in the mental body.

The subconscious mind is seated in the physical and etheric bodies. The etheric body is the unseen energy body that forms the interface between the physical body and other components of the secret anatomy, such as the emotional and mental bodies. Although invisible to the naked eye, the etheric body has a very sophisticated anatomy formed by chakras, or energy vortices, connected through meridians, or energy channels. Chakras and meridians control biological and psychological functions in the body.

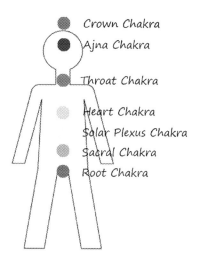

Figure 6. The seven primary chakras

The colors of the seven primary chakras correspond to the colors of dispersed light, which are the colors of the rainbow. The frequencies of the seven colors that form the light spectrum are also similar to those of the primary chakras: the lowest frequency characterizes red, which is the color of the root chakra, and the highest one characterizes violet, which is the color of the crown chakra. As the frequency of the chakras moves up the spinal cord, the frequency of the seven colors of dispersed light also rises from red to violet. This similarity shows that our etheric body displays properties pertaining to light, and that consciousness manifests according to specific light and sound distribution patterns.

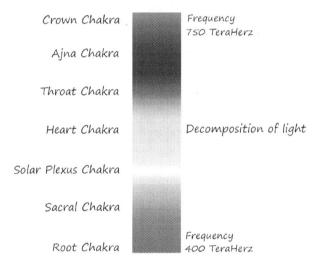

The subconscious mind is one of the components of the unseen software that runs the physical body and dictates external life events. Other intangible components are the emotional and mental bodies.

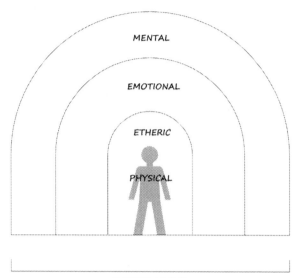

The Conscious Mind versus the Intangible Software

The brain/mind dichotomy can be further explored through oppositions like conscious/subconscious and intangible software/tangible reality. First, let us acknowledge two things: 1) what we see represents barely the tip of the iceberg with regard to what exists, and 2) the subconscious mind, which represents more than 99 percent of the human mind, is not seated in a specific organ, namely the brain.

What we perceive with our five senses is only a tiny fraction of what exists. With our eyes and ears, we can only perceive a limited range of light and sound frequencies. For instance, infrared, ultraviolet, and ultrasound are excluded. There is a reality field that is intangible, and another one that is tangible to us. It is true that our five senses are a window to the world, but because they are a window, they don't allow us to see everything. And when we think that what we don't see does not exist, then we are letting our senses become a limiting prison.

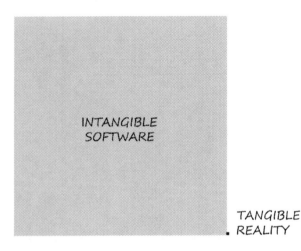

INTANGIBLE
SOFTWARE

TANGIBLE
. REALITY

The subconscious mind and the 99.99 percent void comprised within the human body are intangible to the five senses, whereas more tangible components, such as the conscious mind associated with the brain and the 0.01 particles of matter that form the body, represent only a tiny fraction of reality. Remaining unaware of intangible structures and their impact on human reality is like being an ant sitting on an elephant and commanding it to move; what runs our life is what we don't see, in this instance the elephant.

Consciousness over Matter

What is running the show are nonphysical elements like beliefs, thoughts, and emotions. Despite their nonphysicality, these energies are as real as things; every belief, thought, and emotion is a "code" that shapes reality. They carry an encryption, or energy signature, that impacts both our spiritual and biological anatomies. Thoughts and emotions belong to either love-based or fear-based consciousness. Fear-based thoughts are miscreative and cause distortions in the spiritual and biological anatomies, whereas love-based thoughts are cocreative and do not mutate our original settings, or divine blueprint.

The first step toward empowerment comes with the realization that, rather than being victims of uncontrollable external events, we have the tools to tailor our lives in line with our highest purpose and good. Once the power of thoughts and emotions has been fathomed, along with their role as cocreation tools, then the first step toward healing and mastery has been undertaken. The key role of thoughts and emotions as navigation and manifestation tools is the main tenet of the self-help industry.

If we compare our body and life situation to an airplane, then the intangible software represents the navigation tools. Most are unaware of these tools, so instead of sitting in the pilot's seat, they have delegated their role to an automatic pilot. Getting back in the captain's seat requires acknowledging the role of consciousness as the power that shapes physical reality and beyond. Physical reality as a projection of consciousness is holographic and transitory, whereas consciousness is eternal and forms the fabric of biological and nonbiological life.

How consciousness affects matter on a cellular level has been demonstrated by Dr. Bruce Lipton in his book *The Biology of Belief.* He shows how environmental stimuli impact cellular behavior through the cell's membrane. Lipton considers the membrane to be the mind of the cell, a role previously confined to the DNA. The membrane of the cell contains integral membrane proteins (IMPs) that respond to environmental stimuli and act as fundamental units of awareness and intelligence. There are two types of IMPs: the receptors that read the signals and the effectors that translate the signals into biological behavior. According to Lipton, receptor IMPs read not only physical signals like estrogen or histamine, but also environmental stimuli, such as light, sound, and energy fields.

The membrane of the cell serves as a protective buffer separating the inside of the cell from the environment. Communication with the outside is achieved through the receptor proteins, which act as channels once they are activated by the physical or energetic signals with which they bind. Once activated by environmental stimuli, the receptor proteins are relayed by the effector proteins that translate the signal into biological behavior. This mechanism contributes to the understanding of epigenetics, or how environmental stimuli affect human DNA.

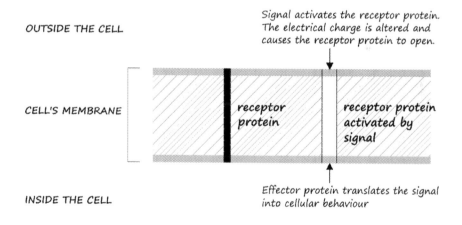

Cellular behavior responds to exogenous stimuli and endogenous programming. Environmental stimuli result from the behavior, as well as the mental and emotional states, of people that we interact with. Endogenous thoughts and emotions come from our inner dialogue, self-image, emotional and mental conditioning, and inner programming.

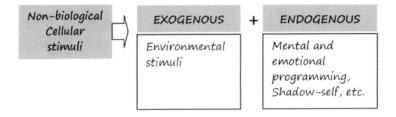

Nonbiological elements, such as external stimuli and inner programming, are continuously influencing the biological behavior of cells.

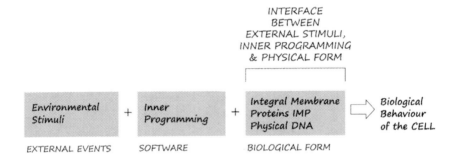

The Role of Emotions

Important components of our intangible anatomy are the mental and emotional bodies. Beliefs and thoughts produced by the mind trigger emotions that have a biological impact. A belief is a recurrent thought that becomes embedded in the mind and ends up forming part of the mental body.

A fear-based belief creates a distortion in the mental body that will be reflected as an undesirable life situation. For example, a distorted core belief about money, such as "money is the root of all evil," will translate as a lack of financial abundance. Since most fear-based beliefs are subconscious, it is hard to fix something that we don't even know exists. Furthermore, conscious fear-based patterns are often justified by self-righteousness: even though judging is fear-based, we feel entitled to judge all the time. Mentally detangling what belongs to fear-based consciousness from what serves our highest good is often a tricky venture.

The role of emotions is to act like pointers. When we hold a thought, the emotion it triggers will indicate whether it is beneficial or detrimental. A thought like "I am not good enough" triggers an unpleasant feeling, indicating that such a belief does not serve our highest purpose. It causes us to contract, whereas a thought like "I am lovable" is accompanied by a feeling of expansion. Negative emotions are warning signs that what we are experiencing is detrimental. Instead of being repressed, they can be used as pointers, indicating when a change in direction needs to be made.

Not only have emotions been denied their role as essential navigation tools, but they have also been deemed shameful. We have always been taught to repress our emotions. This social construct has caused mental distortions to remain uncured, thus becoming transgenerational. It is useful to know two things about emotions: 1) the spectrum of human emotions can be brought down to two basic emotions, love and fear, and 2) emotions are of an energetic nature with physical properties, including a frequency level.

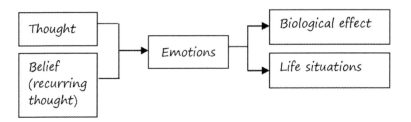

Love versus Fear

There are two basic emotions: love and fear. Emotions that we label as negative stem from fear, and those that we label as positive are expressions of love. Love is a force; it has no opposite. Fear is not the opposite of love—it is only the lack of it. All fear and negativity are degrees of lack of love. This works exactly like darkness and light, with darkness being the absence of light. Light automatically dissipates darkness, which shows that darkness is not the opposite of light, just the lack of it. Light is a power measured in watts and amperes, whereas darkness doesn't have a measuring unit. It only qualifies as the absence of light.

This is what Ronda Byrne, author of *The Secret,* says about love:

"There is no force of negativity. There is only one force, and that force is love. All the negative things you see in the world are always, always manifestations of a lack of love. Whether that negativity is in a person, place, circumstance, or event, it has always come from a lack of love. There isn't a force of sadness; sadness is a lack of happiness, and all happiness comes from love. There isn't a force of failure; failure is a lack of success, and success comes from love. There isn't a force of illness; illness is a lack of health, and all health comes from love. There isn't a force of poverty; poverty is a lack of abundance, and all abundance comes from love. Love is the positive force of life, and any negative condition always comes from a lack of love."

Love as the original language of creation underlying all manifested and unmanifested forms can be defined as the "divine code." When individuation from Source takes place, conscious entities who are granted free will may choose to digress. Digression is the abstinence of love that gives birth to fear. It causes the original settings of the matrix of creation and of the divine blueprint to mutate, thus generating all sorts of dysfunctions. One of them is what we refer to as pain, or suffering, to which the spectrum of negative emotions can be linked.

Emotional Frequency

The spectrum of fear and love-based emotions has been reproduced by Dr. David Hawkins on an emotional frequency scale ranging from zero to 1,000 Hz, where each emotion is represented according to its frequency level. The emotion of courage, calibrating at 200 Hz, separates fear from love-based consciousness.

1000 Hz.....................ENLIGHTENMENT

500 Hz.......................LOVE

200 Hz.......................COURAGE

150 Hz.......................ANGER

100 Hz.......................FEAR

75 Hz.........................GRIEF

30 Hz.........................GUILT

20 Hz.........................SHAME

Below 200 Hz:
Drains energy from others (cords, psychic hooks and attacks etc.)

"In his book Power vs. Force, David Hawkins calibrates people's emotions from 20 to 1,000 Hz, 20 being shame, which is perilously proximate to death. It is destructive to emotional and psychological health and makes us prone to physical illness. At the other end of the scale, at 700–1,000 Hz, is enlightenment.

All levels below 200 are said to be energy-draining and below integrity. These vary from guilt (30), grief (75), fear (100), desire (125), anger (150), up to pride (175). People feel positive as they reach pride level. However, pride feels good only in contrast to the lower levels. Pride is defensive and vulnerable because it is dependent upon external conditions, without which it can suddenly revert to a lower level.

At the 200 level of consciousness, power first appears. Courage (200) is the zone of exploration, accomplishment, fortitude, and determination. People at this level put back into the world as much energy as they take; at the lower levels, populations as well as individuals drain energy from society without reciprocating. Further levels include neutrality

(250), willingness (310), acceptance (350), reason (400) and love (500).

This level is characterized by the development of a love that is unconditional, unchanging, and permanent. It doesn't fluctuate—its source isn't dependent on external factors. Loving is a state of being. It is a forgiving, nurturing, and supportive way of relating to the world. This is the level of true happiness."

Iain, Cindy, Phil, Jeff and the Evolution Team

Two main tipping points can be identified on the emotional frequency scale: 200 Hz, the frequency of courage, and 500 Hz, the frequency of love. A person with an emotional frequency level calibrating below the threshold of 200 Hz is depleted and draining energy from the environment. On the opposite end of the scale is the bandwidth beyond 500 Hz characterized by healing and manifestation, where one becomes an energy provider for the environment.

Anybody situated below 200 Hz is operating mostly in fearmode, and therefore miscreating instead of cocreating. This bandwidth is characterized by struggle, scarcity, and victimhood, as the individual has no control over his environment and thus feels victimized. Anybody situated in this bandwidth is draining energy from society through psychic cords, attacks, or hooks. A quick way of finding out if somebody calibrates below 200 Hz is to assess whether he or she has a physical enemy. Projecting one's own fear-based consciousness on others is a symptom of a dominating shadow-self, which characterizes this particular bandwidth.

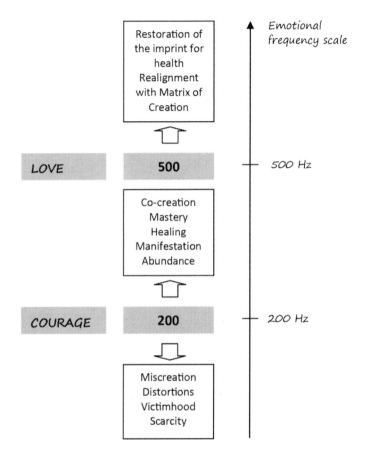

Figure 7. Main tipping points on Dr. Hawkins emotional frequency scale

The Biological Effect of Emotions

Emotions are unseen energies that have tremendous physical effects. How they affect us on a cellular level is the subject of Dr. Masaru Emoto's series of experiments on the reaction of water crystals to emotional stimuli, in which thoughts of anger and of love were directed toward two different samples of water. He thus studied the effect of both love and fear-based emotions on water crystals. The first experiment consisted of a group of people sending simultaneous thoughts of love, such as "you are beautiful," toward a container filled with water. The water crystals were then magnified and photographed. The same experiment was then conducted with thoughts of anger, such as "you make me sick," being directed toward a different water sample.

The results are shown below:

"You are beautiful."   "You make me sick."

More than 60 percent of the human body is made of water. These experiments are only one illustration of how fear-based consciousness is the root of malfunction in the original imprint for health.

Chapter 5
Cocreation versus Miscreation

The Concept of Divine Order

Let us imagine that creation is a game with a set of rules ensuring its proper unfolding. The original game as it was intended by Source comprises the matrix of creation (MC), or the board upon which the game takes place; the divine blueprint (DB), according to which the game of creation is conceived; and divine order (DO), which is the set of rules that include the mechanics of expansion, contraction, and cocreation. DO ensures that creation takes place according to the DB, within the MC.

MC + DB = DO

Iterative miscreation disrupts the divine order, causing a mutation of the divine blueprint, which results in a state of misalignment with the matrix of creation, as well as an underlying chaos disguised as divine order. Despite the fact that reality systems are mainly fear-based, they are disguised as divine order and justified by self-righteousness. The more rigid a reality system is, the bigger the underlying disorder and misalignment with the MC and DB. Dogma is extremely rigid and disguised as divine order, yet it is mainly fear-based, and thus its essence is disorder. The more rigid a reality system appears to be, the bigger is the underlying disorder and misalignment with the MC and DB. The contemporary human race has been operating like this since the beginning of recorded history with no remembrance of a prior order, thus mistaking for divine order reality systems that are built on disorder.

The Consequences of Aligned and Misaligned Consciousness

The free will to cocreate or miscreate has repercussions on the divine blueprint. Every fear-based thought, emotion, and deed causes distortions in the various components of the divine blueprint and an ensuing state of misalignment with the matrix of creation. Distortion and misalignment are the root of what we experience as suffering and pain. Therefore, all the things that we label as negative are a result of the misuse of free will.

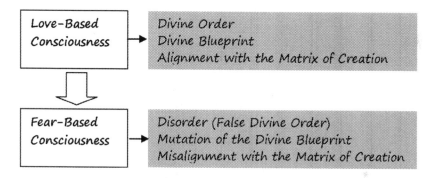

A consciousness aligned with Source operates in love mode, whereas one that is misaligned with Source operates in fear mode, under the illusion of separateness. Misalignment with the matrix of creation entails a mutation of the divine blueprint that blocks the contraction cycle, since distorted consciousness cannot go back to Source and gets stuck in the lower dimensions having to undergo cycles of reincarnation. There isn't an old man sitting on a throne judging us and granting us access to heaven— i.e., higher dimensions and eventually Source. Rather, we are penalizing ourselves through the choices that we make. The fact that we are fully responsible for our own journey is one of the New Age movement's most relevant tenets, as opposed to exoteric religion, in which one is at the mercy of a god that he needs to worship for redemption. The truth is that we are the very emanation of this God-Source, embarked on a journey of cocreation that has led us to where we are, and that we grant ourselves access to heaven when we understand the mechanics of creation and reintegrate our original role as cocreators.

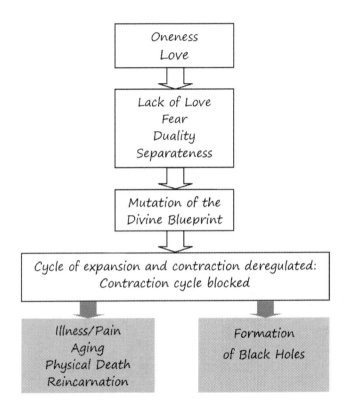

The divine plan is to step down from Source in order to experience creation and to take part in it. Source is the state of oneness, while the stepping-down process entails multiplication and individuation. The law of oneness is meant to federate all creation despite individuation, since all dimensions are intended to be love-based fractal reflections of Source. Infringement on the law of oneness happens through a loss of integrity. A love-based consciousness loses its integrity each time it produces a thought or a deed characterized by a lack of love. The choice to disregard the law of oneness generates a state of lack of love, which gives birth to fear. The natural cycles of expansion and contraction—stepping down from Source and going back to Source—become deregulated, and unnatural processes start to occur, such as death, reincarnation, and even black holes.

The Contemporary Human Template: From Built-in Abilities to Built-in Limitations

After eons of miscreation and iterative reincarnation, the contemporary human template is no longer aligned with its original divine blueprint. It is mutated to the point that the natural cycle of contraction, also called ascension, can no longer take place, leaving souls trapped in the recycling loop of the lower dimensions. Below are some consequences of the mutated human template:

- Loss of natural abilities labeled today as paranormal, including extrasensory perception.
- Embedded fear-based transgenerational programs causing mental, emotional, and physical disorder.
- Deactivation of the DNA and inability to ascend, with aging, physical death, and reincarnation as a result.
- Perceptual confinement to the illusion of physical reality and dictatorship of the "official program."
- Inability to hold multidimensional awareness.
- Inability to manifest.
- Loss of connection with one's inner guidance, higher soul, and Source.
- Creation of unnatural components in the human template, such as the subconscious mind, shadow-self, and negative ego.
- Densification and decay of the human body.
- Oblivion of all the above.

Fear-based consciousness, whether endogenous or exogenous, is one of the primary causes of the misalignment of the human template. Fear-based transgenerational programs are embedded in our DNA, feeding the inorganic subconscious mind, shadow-self, and negative ego and acting like a string of viruses in the mental and emotional bodies. These toxic programs are also embedded within social constructs and mistaken for the ineffable truth or divine order, like the patriarchal value system. These programs dictate behavior and physical reality; they represent a spectrum of cognitive distortions that mislead toward miscreation.

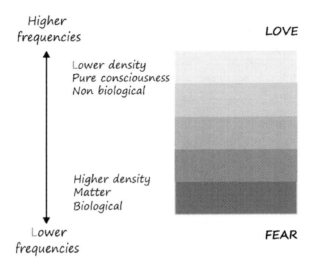

Information is a code. Fear-based programming is disinformation; it is a virus that wreaks havoc in the intangible software. Most people who are unable to make ends meet are unsuspecting of the existence and magnitude of toxic programming, whether transgenerational or learned in the parental context. Everybody's subconscious mind is burdened with fear-based programming, thus making the human template similar to a straitjacket. Built-in abilities have become built-in limitations, hence the "hamster on a wheel" feeling shared by most people.

Successive mutations of the divine blueprint have caused the human body to become denser. Manifestation as dense matter characterizes low levels of consciousness. Furthermore, mutations have caused us to repress the memory of our secret anatomy and purpose, to shut down our inner guidance and to lose our connection with Source.

Fear-Based Morphogenetic Fields and the Perceptual Net

In human biology, morphogenetic fields are groups of cells that form a specific organ. The human embryo comprises these groups of cells that form the liver, lungs, heart, etc. Each morphogenetic field represents the blueprint of a specific organ; for instance, cells in the cardiac field will become heart tissue. Rupert Sheldrake has extended the concept of morphogenetic fields to the nonbiological realm. To every belief, construct, emotion, and behavior corresponds a specific morphogenetic field. The more widespread a belief is, the stronger is its morphogenetic field. After it reaches a critical mass, it starts affecting everyone through morphic resonance, or the hundredth monkey effect.

What is known as the hundredth monkey effect is the result of a study conducted on monkeys by scientists in 1952 on the Japanese island of Koshima. Some monkeys learned how to wash sweet potatoes, and soon this behavior spread to other monkeys through observation. The startling outcome was that after a significant number of monkeys adopted this new behavior, monkeys living on other islands started washing sweet potatoes. Learning how to wash sweet potatoes corresponds to a new behavioral pattern that forms a blueprint, or a morphogenetic field. The more monkeys learned how to wash potatoes, the stronger the morphogenetic field grew, until it reached a tipping point beyond which it was picked up on a psychic level by monkeys on other islands. This illustrates how morphic resonance works: a certain code pertaining to an emotion, a belief, or a behavior is picked up psychically on a collective level after it reaches a critical mass.

Every belief has a morphogenetic field. Let us take a common subconscious belief like "I am not enough." Each time you think you are not enough on a conscious or subconscious level, that thought feeds the morphogenetic field, which grows stronger and ends up affecting others on a mass level through morphic resonance. The morphogenetic field of low self-worth dictates results like scarcity, failure, and obesity. This particular morphogenetic field has become extremely powerful, having been constantly fed for generations, and it now forms a powerful web in which most people are entangled. It is maintained by reality constructs in which one must "do something" in order to "amount to something." This implies that one is by default worthless, unless she proves otherwise by landing a good job, buying a nice car, having offspring, and achieving "success." The feeling of worthlessness by default is further reinforced by the way we have been taught to view our relationship with God as sinners waiting to be saved, as if we are not worthy enough to stand in our own power and acknowledge our godhood.

Spectrum of fear-based emotions and their related morphogenetic fields

SHAME	GUILT	ANGER
Morphogenetic Field of Shame	Morphogenetic Field of Guilt	Morphogenetic Field of Anger

Matrix of fear-based consciousness

Widespread toxic beliefs and distorted social constructs are currently affecting everyone through morphic resonance. Such is the case of the patriarchal value system, the learned scarcity mentality, low self-worth, and the need to compete for love, only to name a few, of which the rat race is a by-product. These distorted constructs form a powerful net dictating cognition and behavior, comparable to the Matrix in the eponym movie, in which the masses have the illusion of free will while being plugged into certain programs. Fear-based morphogenetic fields are comparable to diseased cells that generate anomalies in the matrix of creation.

From Fear-Based Consciousness to Black Hole Systems and the Parallel Matrix

When a divine blueprint crosses the threshold of irreversible mutation, it gets disconnected from the matrix of creation, just like a rotten fruit would fall off a tree. Mutated consciousness that has become disconnected forms what is called the parallel matrix. It exists beyond black holes and sustains itself by draining quanta from other living systems like the Milky Way. Despite its state of misalignment, our galaxy is still connected to the matrix of creation. It forms a closed system characterized by entropy that lies halfway between the matrix of creation and the parallel matrix, and it is being constantly drained through a myriad of black holes.

What is the connection between the mental body and black holes? The mind is the tool by which an individuated consciousness exercises its choice to either cocreate or miscreate. This translates as the will to maintain the integrity of the matrix of creation, or to generate a parallel system by mutating the original one. The saturation of fear-based consciousness in the mental body, leading to an irreversible mutation and a subsequent state of disconnection, explains the connection between the mind and the formation of the parallel matrix. When love-based consciousness gets mutated into fear, a quanta is lost from Source to the parallel matrix. Much emphasis has been placed lately on healing the mind as a way to reclaim one's ability to manifest and to achieve financial success. What we are unsuspecting of is that healing the mind goes far beyond empowerment. It is the doorway to healing the very fabric of creation.

PERSONAL DISTORTIONS		COLLECTIVE DISTORTIONS
Fear-based Mental Body - Conscious mind: Cognitive Distortions - Subconscious mind: Shadow-self Negative Ego	**+** Fear-based Emotional Body	Erosion of Matrix of Creation Formation of Parallel Matrix and Black Hole System

Chapter 6
Evolution versus De-evolution:
Reversal Mode and Black Holes

The Mechanics of Reversal Mode

The contraction cycle that follows every expansion cycle is an evolution. After getting itself fragmented during the stepping-down process, a consciousness evolves back to Source by accreting frequency and pulling together all its individuated parts. Miscreation causes the evolution process to become a de-evolution. This state characterizes a consciousness that has mutated to the point where it can no longer evolve back to Source. It remains stuck, forming parallel systems that are continuously draining quanta from the matrix of creation in order to sustain themselves.

The merkaba surrounding a body, or a planet, consists of two electrical and electromagnetic fields that spin in opposite directions to one another, thus creating a vortex that not only allows for transdimensional travel, but also represents a vital link to the matrix of creation. In the case of an individuated consciousness operating in reversal mode, the fields spin in the opposite direction to an organic merkaba. An activated organic merkaba is an ascension vortex, whereas an inorganic one is a black hole vortex drawing energy from the environment. This process illustrates the mechanics by which quanta is drained from the matrix of creation. The alteration of the divine blueprint that causes the merkaba to spin in reverse has two results: not only does the individuated consciousness become disconnected from the matrix of creation, but it also starts draining quanta from it. Hence, parallel systems formed eons ago have had an unceasing domino effect on the erosion of the matrix of creation. The fall described in the Bible is part of that erosion process.

Where do we fit in all this? The Milky Way is in a state of misalignment with the matrix of creation; therefore, the contraction cycle has been blocked for hundreds of thousands of years. It is subject to entropy because the mutation of the divine blueprint hinders the proper flow of energy from Source, and also because its quanta is constantly being drained into the parallel matrix through black holes. Their gravitational pull is so strong that they have been called the drains of the universe. The size of the black hole located at the center of the Milky Way is believed to amount to more than three million times the size of our sun. It is called a supermassive black hole and is constantly increasing in size, so as to threaten the entire galaxy.

The Consequences of Misalignment: Entropy and Vampirism

Two consequences of the state of misalignment with the matrix of creation are entropy and vampirism, with the second one being the unnatural remedy to the first. Our galaxy, planet, and physical body are entropic systems that we will refer to as closed systems. Understanding these mechanics is crucial for us to fathom what is at stake and to reach a clear assessment of the purpose of our presence on earth. Theoretical perspectives provided by the religious, philosophical, and scientific paradigms omit these two important facts: 1) our system is closed because of the many distortions it comprises, with two major results that are entropy and vampirism, and 2) the main purpose of anybody who finds himself in a closed system is to restore the imprint for health, in order to be able to engage in the contraction/ascension cycle.

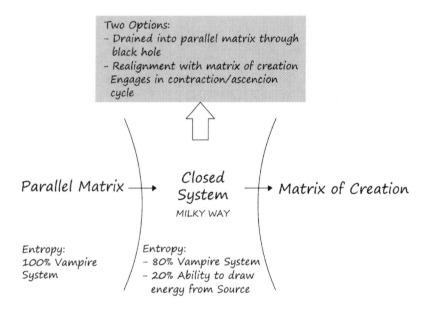

Closed systems are fallen systems. When consciousness becomes distorted through iterative miscreation, the properties of its divine blueprint mutate. Let us say that the matrix of creation is made of water, and the distorted blueprint of consciousness transforms into oil—water and oil don't match. The fall described in the Bible was provoked by the mechanics of creation rather than by the wrath of an angry creator. Our entire galaxy fell from a higher dimension because of excessive miscreations that caused disruptions in the matrix of creation, provoking parts of it to collapse. We are not the center of the universe nor the only species, as we tend to think. We are here because of previous miscreations that took place even before our existence as a human race.

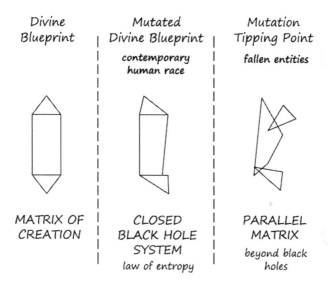

The parallel matrix is a vampire system feeding off closed systems that are still connected to the matrix of creation. The erosion process takes place when love-based consciousness is transmuted into fear. The drama-based media and the dog-eat-dog world where individuals live in a constant state of fear are supporting this process. The mental body plays a crucial role when it comes to restoring the imprint for health by reverse-mutating fear into love. A healed divine blueprint is the key that opens the exit door from distorted systems back to Source. The myth of going to heaven is that of exiting our closed system.

Reversal Mode and Vampirism

Once an entity enters reversal mode, vampirism becomes its only survival mode. This unnatural process allows a disconnected entity to form an artificial connection to the matrix of creation in order to avoid total depletion, since its quanta is finite and cannot be replenished. Psychic cords and hooks are the inorganic tools used to replace the broken spiritual cord that previously formed a natural connection to Source.

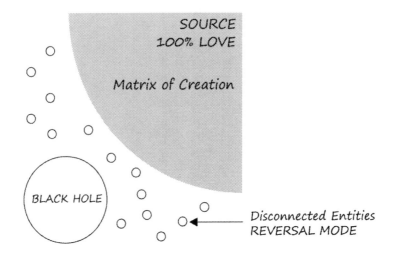

As compensation for depletion, individuals operating in fear mode draw energy from the environment in the form of psychic hooks and cords, more commonly known as psychic attacks. This process is comparable to symbiosis, where an organism uses a plant as an illegal host from which it draws vital energy. There are two types of vampires, disconnected entities operating in reversal mode, and connected entities operating in fear mode and therefore depleted.

Earth and earthlings are an easy prey for fallen entities from the parallel matrix for two reasons: 1) their location in a black hole system populated with such entities and 2) their connection to the matrix of creation, which still allows them to supply themselves with energy despite the fact that they are in a closed system subject to entropy.

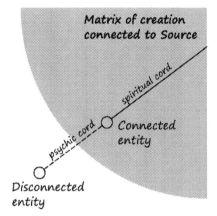

A closed system like ours has the following characteristics: it is misaligned but still connected to the matrix of creation; it is a vampire system with predators and prey; and it is being vampirized by disconnected systems like the parallel matrix. With vampirism as the predominant survival mode, disempowerment to the extent of enslavement has been and continues to be an essential tool for producing easy prey on a mass level.

Part II

The Energetic Harness:
Reality as a Prison

You have to understand—most people are not ready to be unplugged, and many of them are so inured, so hopelessly dependent on the system, that they will fight to protect it.

Morpheus in The Matrix

Chapter 1
The Fall and Mission Planet Earth

The Principle of Free Will

One of the basic rules of creation is the principle of free will as more and more entities individuate from a master soul during the stepping-down process and dimensions are formed like ripples on the water. Individuated souls incarnated in dimension n form one spiritual entity in a higher dimension $n+1$, until a state of oneness is reached near Source. Free-will choices and deeds that contradict the initial state of oneness are acts of miscreation.

The purpose of creation and the divine plan is cocreation. Consciousness individuates progressively from an initial state of oneness and is given the opportunity to participate in the creation process. An expansion cycle is comparable to a musical event where everybody joins efforts to achieve a common purpose of cocreation, which is creating and experiencing joy, at the end of which everybody goes home. Miscreation occurs when free will is misused. An example would be terrorists attacking the concert venue and not letting people out. After a while, those who are trapped become oblivious of who they are and what they came here to do, and they start adopting a fearful and chaotic behavior, miscreating themselves.

Although it is a universal law, cocreation is not enforced, it is maintained by free will. Enforcement is a measure that cannot possibly apply in a love-based universe, as it is a form of disempowerment and limitation of responsibility. Love-based consciousness is a state of godhood that does not tolerate any form of restriction.

Miscreation and the Fall

Miscreation is an act of free will exercised by an individuated consciousness in misalignment with Source. It impacts simultaneously the divine blueprint on an individual level and the matrix of creation on a wider scale. It causes love-based divine consciousness to be transmuted into fear-based consciousness with its corollary spectrum of negative thoughts and emotions. After an individuated consciousness crosses a mutation threshold, its distortions start affecting the matrix of creation. When a divine blueprint mutates to a point where it gets disconnected, an erosion of the matrix of creation takes place, which consists of the translocation of quanta from Source to the parallel matrix.

Repeated cycles of miscreation have caused the Milky Way galaxy, including our solar system, to fall from a higher dimension where consciousness takes an etheric rather than a gross matter form. Although it fell from a higher dimension, earth is still connected to the matrix of creation and withholds the potential to ascend back to its original position.

Mission Planet Earth

Speculation about the origins and purpose of the human race is endless, whether scientific, religious, spiritual, or philosophical. Speculation is the result of oblivion. When an essential body of information related to the origin and purpose of our race goes missing, the role of speculative theories, often dressed as dogma or scientific facts, is to fill in the gap.

How about a new theory? The presence of the human race is much prior to recorded history, and what the scientific paradigm would have us believe. What if instead of evolving haphazardly from apes and sea creatures, we were engineered in the image of God, i.e., according to a divine blueprint? Introducing the human race that holds the divine blueprint into a misaligned system is like injecting a vital serum into a dying organism. This analogy gives a broad idea of why our race originated in a distorted system. It also explains our eternal quest for heaven or nirvana, as if we knew on a subconscious level that a better place existed. This Promised Land is religion's most valuable indoctrination tool.

The original human race holding the divine blueprint started its journey on earth eons ago in order to accomplish a specific mission, which is to bring into realignment this fallen part of the matrix of creation. Over the course of a long history that is unknown to the contemporary human race, our divine blueprint became distorted until we forgot our true origins and purpose. We now think that our distressed planet is the center of the universe and that our ancestors are apes.

Life on planet earth started as a rescue mission. Mission Planet Earth is primarily an ascension mission.

Chapter 2
The Journey from Gods to Dogs

Not Exactly in God's Image

Prehistory is science's official viewpoint on the origin and evolution of the human race. Hominids evolved from the genus *Homo,* leading to the appearance of *Homo sapiens,* known as the ancestor of our contemporary human race. In other words, our race evolved from very primitive hominid creatures, like the *Homo habilis,* who is the first ancestor known to have used stone tools 2.3 million years ago. Three myths of our origins coexist: 1) the scientific viewpoint known as prehistory, 2) the religious belief that God created the universe between Monday and Saturday and then took Sunday off, and 3) theories about advanced races like the Atlantean civilization, known as pseudohistory. All three seem to be highly contradictory, but what if they could be reconciled? The theory of a previous advanced race may not be pure elucubration, since the original human race enjoyed abilities and powers that are the attributes of an intact divine blueprint and that qualify today as supernatural. Between the existence of this original race and the evolution of our contemporary race from the *Homo habilis,* something must have happened. This severe mutation of the divine blueprint can only be the result of the introduction of fear-based consciousness, which translates as miscreation on an endogenous level and ill-intended manipulation on an exogenous one.

If we agree that creation follows a love-based divine blueprint, then we can ascertain that there was an original human race exempt from fear-based dysfunctions. Reckoning that the individuation of consciousness follows a perfectly ordered love-based pattern is much more plausible than the haphazard evolution viewpoint. Since everything that functions well requires order, we cannot assume that the underlying principle of creation relies on a haphazard theory, but rather on precise mechanics. Chaos is the result of a virus, in this instance fear-based consciousness transmuting organic into inorganic light, thus generating a string of dysfunctions. These can be severe to the point of causing a fragmentation of consciousness; hence, it is equally plausible that fear-based consciousness can mutate the original settings of an advanced race to the point where it has to evolve back from hominids.

The coexistence of advanced races like the Atlanteans around 10,000 BC with less evolved forms of consciousness that had been evolving from *Homo sapiens* for 200,000 years is comparable to the discrepancies that exist today between the human race and the animal kingdom, which is a less evolved form of consciousness. Because energy is always in motion, the downgrading and upgrading of consciousness is constant and obeys precise mechanics.

Covert Manipulations and Dark Agendas

Humans were designed as an enlightened and powerful race entrusted with a noble mission. One of the reasons we are not that race anymore is because of external manipulations orchestrated by entities that have been operating in reversal mode even before the fall of the Milky Way. The interest of these entities, or fallen races, in us is manifold: 1) we are located in a black hole system that they can access; 2) we are connected to the matrix of creation—although we fell—so we represent a vital supply of energy and a bridge to the living universe; and 3) some groups covet earth as a planet that they can colonize and use for their own evolution, as an upgrade from their current location.

These fallen races whose consciousness has reached a critical misalignment with Source, so as to become intentionally opposed to the law of oneness, have been interfering with earthly affairs prior to the beginning of recorded history. The result has been severe mutations in the human spiritual and biological anatomies, causing a loss of natural abilities that are today labeled as extrasensory and paranormal and the oblivion of our origins and mission. They are also behind the embedding of cognitive distortions within religious and social constructs, such as the imbalance between masculine and feminine and the dichotomy between science and spirituality, as well as a myriad of disempowering mind viruses disguised as god-given value systems.

Through manipulation and accumulated fear-based consciousness, the human template has become what it is today: a disempowering straitjacket. The human experience is one of limitations, illness, aging, death, and reincarnation. Another ability that humans have lost is their ability to ascend back to Source. Not only are most people caught up in the drama of their lives like hamsters on a wheel, they are also condemned to an eternal "Groundhog Day" through the endless reincarnation cycle.

The covert disempowerment agenda exists because other races operating in reversal mode have interest in sabotaging the realignment mission and harnessing the human race as energetic quanta to be preyed on. Why would a hungry lion let prey pass him by? The more we deny the existence of these other races by claiming that it is not yet a scientific truth, or because the religious paradigm does not allow for such a theory, the more disempowered we remain. Information is power. Misinformation, and therefore disempowerment, has made us easy prey. But we have certainly reached a point in our evolution where many of us are starting to sense a different truth beyond the limiting mind viruses that have been informing our reality constructs so far.

Sabotaged Ascension and the Vicious Circle

When an expansion cycle ends, it is followed by a contraction cycle. This natural process has been blocked on earth for eons; whenever the contraction cycle is deemed to start, or when the party ends and it's time to go home, the mutated part cannot go back. We can compare the divine blueprint of the individuated forms of consciousness evolving in our system to water that mutation has caused to transform into oil. We know that water and oil don't mix because of their different physical properties. Fallen and misaligned parts of the matrix of creation, because of severe mutations, have now transformed into oil and cannot undertake the contraction cycle, or going back home to water. Therefore, the human mission, which is "Mission Ascension," has failed repeatedly, keeping the rescued and their rescuers trapped in a vicious cycle of stationary evolution, entailing an endless recycling of consciousness within a closed system. Sabotaging Mission Ascension is the agenda of fallen races from the parallel matrix. The term "dark agenda" associated with the Illuminati is now quite familiar. Sabotaging Mission Ascension is what underlies the so-called dark agenda; the "New World Order" is merely the tip of the iceberg of what is really at stake.

Chapter 3
The Purpose of Enslavement

Reversal Mode and the Origins of Chaos

The consequence of reversal mode is that a conscious entity gets disconnected from the matrix of creation: it falls. After the fall occurs, the disconnected entity is left with finite quanta of energy that cannot be replenished, just like a fallen leaf can no longer receive sap from the tree. Consequently, the fall leads to the fragmentation of the individuated form of consciousness.

So far, the mechanics of reversal mode make sense. When a consciousness mutates so as to fall, the logical sequence is that it gets rejected from the matrix of creation, just like a diseased cell would be rejected from a living organism. It then implodes and reintegrates the matrix of creation as fragmented pieces of consciousness recyclable within Source. These mechanics ensure that the consequences of the misuse of free will can be contained through the rejection of mutated entities and their subsequent recycling as splintered units of consciousness. Except something went wrong, and then many things started going wrong.

What did go wrong? Not only did fallen entities seek ways to avoid implosion, but they also decided to establish a parallel inorganic order that they sustain by preying on the matrix of creation. It is an established fact that our galaxy is being progressively drained into the black hole located at its center, in addition to the myriad of black holes that it contains, rightly called the drains of the universe. This illegitimate fight for survival is the premise of chaos in this part of the universe where earth is stationed and beyond. Its episodes are more hallucinatory than the most flamboyant sci-fi movie.

Humans as Energy Supply

The advantage that reversal-mode entities have over contemporary humanity is their knowledge of the mechanics of creation and of the history of this universe, whereas we live inside a syncretic myth forged by religious dogma, social value systems, and other constructs like Cartesianism, positivism, capitalism, consumerism, etc. Therefore, an important component of the dark agenda has always been to conceal the mechanics of creation and cocreation. It is no surprise that the basic alphabet of mental and emotional mastery has been called "The Secret": it is indeed unknown to the masses and barely scratches the surface of humanity's lost body of knowledge.

Preying on the matrix of creation is an erosion process during which love-based consciousness is deprived of love, thus becoming fear-based. The mutation of love-based consciousness happens through the mind, subsequently affecting the emotional body. Hence, embedding mental viruses and toxic programs on a collective level represents a powerful erosion tool. Such cognitive distortions that establish what is "right" from what is "wrong" pervade social systems; only a few decades ago did the sacredness of feminine virginity start appearing to some as unsubstantial. Just think of how much suffering this taboo has caused throughout the ages and how many crimes this cognitive distortion has justified. This shows the stronghold of mental viruses on the masses and how distorted consciousness can actually be dressed as a god-given truth.

Miscreation driven by fear-based consciousness chisels away at the matrix of creation, and the more eroded it gets, the more its parts get disconnected and fall—thus reinforcing the parallel matrix. Fear-based programs, thoughts, emotions, and deeds are powerful erosion tools. The parallel matrix can be compared to a hungry monkey and the matrix of creation to a coconut tree: the hungry monkey will not stop shaking the tree until it loses all its fruit. Entities operating in reversal mode remedy their isolation from Source by establishing inorganic and illegitimate connections through other forms of consciousness that are still connected to the living matrix. Psychic cords, hooks, and attacks are the tools that are commonly used to establish these inorganic connections.

These dysfunctions remain confined to the lower dimensions, since fallen entities cannot access higher realms because of their inorganic blueprint. Their physical properties no longer match the requirements of love-based dimensions in terms of the nature of the atoms, frequency, and ARPS. Access to "heaven" does not hinge upon an old man, but rather on individual choices made in terms of cocreation and miscreation. The myth of the old man granting access to heaven is yet another deeply rooted cognitive distortion keeping the mental body locked into a state of misperception and dysfunction. Ironically, buying into this misperception is a good guarantee not to see heaven, as responsibility is relinquished and the true mechanics of creation and cocreation are not understood.

Hybridization and the Illuminati

Who are the entities operating in reversal mode who are keeping us energetically harnessed and using us as food? This is the point where things start to seem like science fiction, especially because we are used to thinking that we are the only race in the universe. One of the objectives of the dark agenda is that we remain misinformed by thinking that we are the only race, and that whoever claims otherwise be discredited and labeled as mentally deranged.

Because fallen entities operate under the complete dominion of their ego, they are referred to as "service-to-self." Most of them have certainly reached a point of no return in their inorganic mutation—their emotional bodies have become so atrophied that they can no longer experience compassion or any other emotion. Zombies are unfortunately not a mere product of our imagination.

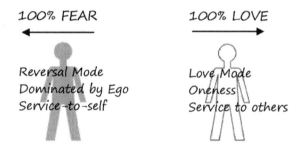

Figure 8. The concept of service-to-self

The first time an entity shifted to reversal mode after a certain level of miscreation is impossible for us to pinpoint. However, it certainly happened long before the creation of the Milky Way, this galaxy being the by-product of a fall provoked by the mechanics of reversal mode. Several fallen races have been meddling with human affairs, using wormholes to access our physical dimension. Hybridization of the service-to-self with humans has occurred in times much prior to the beginning of recorded history, and it continues to take place. The presence of these alien codes in our nonbiological DNA template is variable. The Illuminati, who hold a higher proportion of the mutated DNA, are working covertly to achieve the objectives of the dark agenda. This may not sound plausible to many readers. There is no obligation to believe this theory; being aware of it as a probability is sufficient. Although the Illuminati represent a rather small proportion of earth's population, they have dominion over the political and financial arenas and are covertly manipulating many other important institutions.

Chapter 4
Dysfunctions of the Human Template

DNA Deactivation and Other Dysfunctions of the Secret Anatomy

The template of contemporary humanity has strayed from the original divine blueprint, having undergone several mutation cycles throughout the course of an uncharted history. Dysfunctions pervade all levels of the secret anatomy, including the geometric template, nonbiological DNA, the merkaba vehicle, and the mental, emotional, etheric, and physical bodies. These dysfunctions are behind the formation of inorganic components like the shadow-self and negative ego. The human template is now misaligned to the point that every individual who incarnates on this planet will show some sort of dysfunction on the mental, emotional, etheric, and physical levels. Hospitals and the pharmaceutical industry, for instance, are not-so-gentle reminders of this underlying truth.

Dysfunctions that affect the nonbiological and biological DNA have caused most of the initial twelve strands to become dormant, thus incurring a monumental loss in natural abilities and triggering a three-dimensional lock that creates a perceptual confinement to physical reality. The fewer activated strands of DNA, the less consciousness and frequency that can be accreted. Therefore, information with a high frequency encryption cannot be processed by a system functioning with only a few active strands of DNA. A high amount of deactivated DNA can be compared to a high ratio of closed windows as opposed to open ones, meaning that less information beyond the official paradigm seeps through. Dysfunctional DNA also blocks ascension, since this operation requires all the components of the spiritual anatomy to be fully operational. The small amount of information that can be processed by contemporary humanity translates as a state of amnesia and a perceptual confinement to the single perspective of the official paradigm.

The Relationship between Toxic Programming, Mental Distortions, and Karma

The contribution of toxic programming to the dysfunction of the human template is mainly twofold: it generates distortions in the mental body that trickle down to the rest of the intangible and physical anatomies, and it anchors fear-based consciousness and inorganic light. The result is a divine blueprint that operates in a state of misalignment with the matrix of creation.

Negative programming is a defective code, or a virus wreaking havoc in the nonbiological and biological anatomies. It is the root of negative life events and situations. What toxic programming does is create cognitive distortions. How can you undertake the right course of action if what you perceive is a deformed perspective? How can you cocreate if you are being mislead? Toxic programming is the root of miscreation that generates karma. There is a correlation between transgenerational, parental, and social toxic programming and what is referred to as karma, i.e., a set of distortions that keep repeating themselves like a vicious circle, driving a person to miscreate and thus generating additional karma.

Fear-based Negative Belief:
"I am not good enough"

External events reinforce the fear-based belief

Fear-based belief provokes external events in line with itself

Mental distortions are both transgenerational and acquired throughout life. The inherited set of toxic beliefs is usually aggravated by mental distortions present in the parental and social contexts. This accumulated baggage will cause the individual to miscreate, thus increasing furthermore the weight of negative karma.

Karma accumulated throughout a lifetime by adding transgenerational, parental, and social mental distortions to personal miscreations translates as inorganic light that mutates the divine blueprint, thus preventing the next stage in the contraction cycle from taking place. Mental and emotional distortions play an essential role in the mechanics of "the wheel of karma."

Mental distortion is another word for fear-based consciousness. Each negative thought is the starting point of a vicious circle, as it codes external events in line with itself that will in turn feed this belief. It is the reason why people reproduce the same patterns, and their life ends up like *Groundhog Day.* They are usually unaware of the cause, too busy blaming external events and bad luck. They don't know that their life situation is the effect of an intangible cause that is seeking attention, healing, and release. Fortunately, toxic programming is something that one has not only the ability, but also the responsibility to heal.

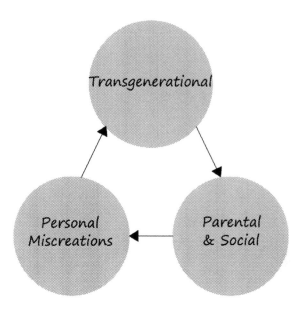

Figure 9. Vicious circle of mental distortions, or wheel of karma

Breaking free of the wheel of karma is achieved by healing the mental body; the doorway out of the closed system is through the mind. It is the reason why the mechanics of enslavement rely mostly on implementing and maintaining mind viruses. The mental distortions they create form an energetic prison and a perceptual net that sabotage the contraction/ascension cycle, just like a stick would block a wheel, preventing it from moving forward. The challenge of restoring the imprint for health is that mental distortions are often disguised as the "right values," and failure to comply with them is usually punished by shame and social exclusion. Misperception is the primary obstacle that stands in the way of correcting mental distortions.

Unconscious Parenting: How Words Create Worlds

Toxic programming is transgenerational, parental, and social. Unconscious parenting is extremely harmful since children act like psychic sponges and are deeply imprinted with the information received from the environment. This information combined with other transgenerational programs forms software that will code their physical reality. Unconscious parenting is the act of planting the seeds of a defective code that will be mirrored later as negative life situations and experienced as painful limitations.

Although a lot of emphasis has been placed on good parenting, there remains a need for constant self-monitoring, as a lot of seemingly innocent statements like "Wash your hands—you are dirty!" can have devastating effects on a child's self-image and interpretation of his or her own self-worth. The undetected negative impact of a seemingly innocent and legitimate statement can be so drastic as to dictate failure, obesity, scarcity, etc.

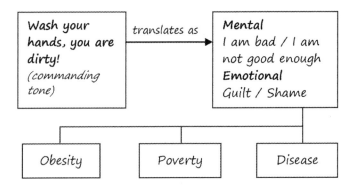

Most legitimate parental language is strongly contributing to planting the seeds of the good/bad duality. Children have to comply with so many rules and constantly fulfill their parents' wishes in order not to be labeled as "bad." Bad translates as unlovable, and that is everybody's worst fear.

The consequence of the misuse of the good/bad duality is that from an early age, children are constantly made to feel bad about themselves. Because this feeling is unnatural and painful, it is repressed in the subconscious mind, thus forming the shadow-self and its corollary, the negative ego. It translates as the need to be better, to compete for love by having more money, beauty, success, or toys, or to belittle others in order to feel good about oneself. The result is a dog-eat-dog society.

Feeling bad/unlovable → *repressed in subconscious* → *forms the shadow-self* → *forms the negative ego* → *need to compete for love* → *contributes to the creation of the dog eat dog world.*

Some common toxic programs are:

Toxic Program Cognitive Distortion	Truth
You are flawed by default and need to do such-and-such in order to be accepted: do your homework, make your bed, be quiet, keep your clothes clean, do as we say, be who we want you to be, etc.	You are worthy by default and an expression of the divine.
Resources are scarce and money doesn't grow on trees, hence the need to struggle.	Abundance, manifestation, and playfulness are everybody's birthright.
You are not enough and need to compete for love.	You are perfectly loveable and deserve unconditional love.

Life is about struggle and survival. Marriage, offspring, and material possessions are the ultimate goals; if you don't achieve these goals, you will be rejected and made to feel flawed.	Life is about healing, cocreation, spiritual actualization, and ascension.
The search for God is external.	The search for God is an internal journey.
You are disempowered by default and the victim of external events and life situations.	You are the master of your own reality and empowered by acknowledging your godhood.
Learn to judge yourself and others and to position yourself with regard to others in the struggle/survival paradigm.	Acknowledge yourself and others.
It is normal to age, get sick, and die.	Aging, ailment, and death are the result of miscreation.

Unconscious parenting is the process of educating children to miscreate by seeding toxic programs, therefore aggravating karma and dysfunction. The ultimate result is spiritual entrapment as a consequence of the mutation of the divine blueprint. Unconscious parenting is quantity-oriented, whereas conscious parenting is focused on restoring the imprint for health, achieving freedom from the energetic harness, and spiritual actualization.

Unconscious Parenting	Conscious Parenting
- Emphasis on multiplication - Aggravation of distortions - Spiritual entrapment - Energetic harnessing	- Emphasis on healing - Restoration of the divine blueprint - Spiritual actualization - Restoration of the potential for ascension

The Good/Bad Duality and the Formation of the Negative Ego

The misused good/bad duality is at the core of religious, social, and educational systems. The premise of all these constructs is that one needs to engage in all sorts of undertakings in order to feel worthy and accepted, and to avoid being labeled as bad. If we were to acknowledge our godhood, despite the present mutations of the human template, we would realize that our systems are rooted in falsehood and that our perception of ourselves has been deformed since early childhood. In the good/bad paradigm, each time a person is made to feel bad about himself because he or she didn't accomplish something or behave in a certain way, the shadow-self and negative ego become inflated. Their role is to compensate for the "I am bad" feeling, thus generating behavioral and emotional distortions.

The good/bad duality is a dangerous tool that can be manipulated to legitimize fear-based behavior, feed self-righteousness, and foster judgment and the illusion of separateness. Wars and terrorism are rooted in self-righteousness: "We are right to fight against what is wrong." The need to label things as good or bad is an act of judging, and judging is not loving. It is a fear-based behavior rooted in the illusion of separateness. If the primary intent behind the good/bad duality is to promote goodness as the ultimate quest, then its misuse is creating converse effects.

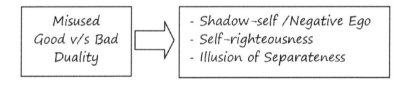

Chapter 5
Polarization and Imbalances

The Imbalance between Masculine and Feminine

Masculine and feminine energies are meant to balance and complement each other. The result of one type of energy dominating the other is the creation of reality constructs like the patriarchal value system. Such an imbalanced construct promotes values like an inflated ego, separateness, hierarchy, and oppression. The result is a stifled self-expression and an aborted self-actualization, as the individual is made to comply with the dogmas and strict rules of the social group to which he belongs. This reality construct with its body of cognitive distortions is typical of patriarchal societies worldwide until the second half of the twentieth century, which marks a return of the "feminine" shunned since the beginning of recorded history.

Patriarchal societies derive from the imbalance between masculine and feminine, which they strive to maintain through a rigid value system. This is achieved mainly by manipulating the good/bad duality, where values that maintain the imbalance are labeled as right—for instance, feminine virginity. Labeling something as right and its opposite as wrong is a powerful mind-control tool used successfully for centuries. This is evidenced by the fact that it took humanity thousands of years of evolution to achieve a partial restoration of individual and feminine rights, and only on some parts of the planet.

Social and religious constructs are based on an imbalance of the masculine/feminine duality as well as a misuse of the good/bad duality. The imbalance between masculine and feminine is the root of falsehood in social and religious constructs. The role of the good/bad duality is to legitimize this imbalance, by labeling as right the values that reinforce it. The ultimate purpose of creating imbalances is to seed on a mass level mental distortions that promote fear-based consciousness, thus maintaining a state of misalignment with the matrix of creation.

The Imbalance between Logic and Intuition

Logic is known to be an attribute of the left side of the brain, whereas the right side is the seat of intuition and emotion. Reason and logic are rooted in the linearity of time and space. Edison failed hundreds of times before inventing the light bulb; electricity has been there all along, but because of linearity, it took hundreds of years to harness this power. Linearity is bypassed by combining intuition with logic. Many scientific breakthroughs are the fruit of intuition; for instance, the structure of biological DNA was envisioned by Watson following an intake of recreational drugs. Logic and intuition are built-in navigation and cocreation tools designed to work together and complement each other. Successful entrepreneurs are familiar with the trick of using both logic and intuition and have relied on this combined tool to achieve astounding results.

Intuition is usually labeled as non-scientific. The result is silenced inner guidance and unacknowledged emotions. Repressing intuition and emotion curtails the cognition of the subconscious mind, thus keeping the doorway to healing the shadow-self closed. Furthermore, it keeps all cognition subject to the linearity of logic, therefore significantly reducing our perceptual abilities. Logic and intuition are tools that complement each other, just like the right and left hands are both needed in order to be able to clap.

The Imbalance between Science and Spirituality

The logic-intuition dichotomy underlies the antagonism between science and spirituality. Reason and logic are the tools of science, confined to explaining the laws of physical reality, recognized as the only reality. The issue of existence before birth and after death is labeled as metaphysical and tackled by religion, esoteric and New Age movements, and philosophical speculation. What if there was one body of scientific laws governing the physical and metaphysical realms, and what if these two realms were inseparable and the extension of one another?

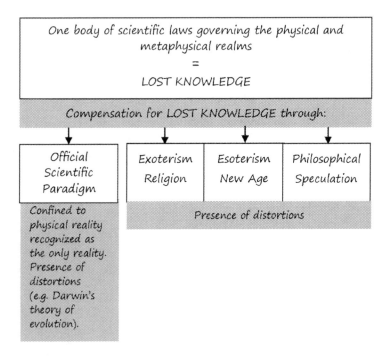

Antagonizing the physical and metaphysical realms creates an opposition between their respective tools "reason-logic" and "faith-intuition," thus making logic and intuition appear contradictory rather than complementary. The fake opposition between these two complementary tools hinders the process of understanding the mechanics of our universe. Putting together the pieces of the puzzle cannot be achieved without a prior realization that the separation between the physical and metaphysical realms is illusionary. The common belief that science is only relevant in the physical realm cannot be farther from the truth, since the invisible mechanics of creation obey very specific scientific laws and have measurable biological effects. Physical and metaphysical realities are governed by one set of scientific laws, allowing for the first to become an expression of the second. Just like our physical body is not random, neither is our intangible anatomy and the nonphysical realm. The mechanics of creation and cocreation are the science of the unseen. Not only do the science of the unseen and the science of the seen—i.e., official science—complement each other, but they also overlap, and official science is now taking baby steps toward explaining the laws of the unseen through the lens of quantum physics.

The makeup of complementary couples as antagonisms creates dysfunctional reality constructs; for instance, the patriarchal value system anchors fear-based consciousness, and Cartesianist and positivist societies are forever imprisoned in the pragmatism of official reality, and therefore condemned to a state of perceptual confinement. Correcting the dichotomy misperception by realizing that masculine and feminine, logic and emotion, science and religion work together is essential for putting the pieces of the puzzle together. Widespread fake dichotomies are in reality cognitive distortions preventing us from regaining the knowingness that was once our birthright, and they are ultimately sabotaging Mission Ascension. They are the pillars of our present paradigm and the foundations of the construct that forms official reality.

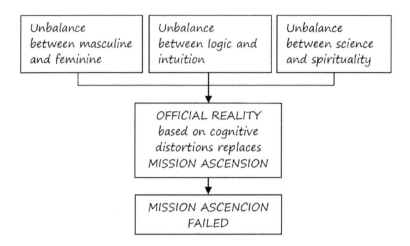

Science without religion is lame, religion without science is blind.

Albert Einstein

Chapter 6
The Construct of Reality

Religion's Side Effects

Our cognition of reality is a syncretism of religious, spiritual, philosophical, scientific, and social constructs. The interpretation that modern society gives of the origins of mankind is based on a combination of Darwin's theory of evolution and religious dogma. This example illustrates how the construct of reality meshes science, religion, philosophy, social traditions, and value systems, in addition to economic modes of production that determine lifestyles. Since distortion pervades all these components, it is not overstated to say that the end product forms a convex mirror reflecting a deformed image of reality.

Religious value systems stem from two main unbalanced polarizations that they actively seek to maintain: the masculine/feminine imbalance that anchors fear-based consciousness and the good/bad duality manipulated so as to legitimize the first imbalance by qualifying as "right" whatever reinforces it. Dogma that contradicts the true mechanics of creation and cocreation includes the personification of God as a male figure; "he" is a consciousness pervading all creation, since all particles and antiparticles originate from this Source. Even mutated consciousness originates from Source and gets recycled within it, so nothing is permanently outside the universal consciousness referred to as God.

If we are a fractal manifestation of God, then how come we feel so helpless? The answer is that we have been fed disempowering beliefs for eons, like the need to bow in front of icons and statues. Why would God want us to bow or kneel? Would you want to see your son or daughter bow or kneel in front of you, or would you rather like to see them empowered and full of self-respect?

The embedding of misaligned concepts within religion creates distortions in the mental body that have mutating effects on the divine blueprint:
-   The victim/sinner mentality, or the seed of disempowerment. It breeds low self-worth, indirectly driving the need to compete for love and worthiness.

- Promoting the external search for the sacred and divine, which is equivalent to teaching someone to look for something in the opposite direction.
- Relinquishing responsibility to an external power, thus blocking the doorway to mastery, spiritual actualization, and ascension.
- Occulting the true mechanics of creation and cocreation, such as denying the existence of the secret anatomy, multidimensionality, etc.

These constructs distort the true mechanics of creation, thus driving the individual to miscreate, maintaining or aggravating the state of misalignment of the divine blueprint and ultimately blocking ascension. As compensation, the religious paradigm provides two major ersatz: 1) the "going to heaven" myth and a false prescription as to how it is achieved, and 2) the "official program" or universal recipe for happiness. Although religions may promote love-based concepts such as forgiveness, compassion, and tithing, they are mainly in a state of misalignment with the matrix of creation. Discernment is advisable, as one cannot expect to be given a preconceived set of ideas to follow without questioning the very nature of these precepts and asking how they may serve him to his highest potential and truth.

Abducting Jesus

Misperceptions of God also extend to prophets. The ideology and dogma built around the persona of a prophet can contradict his message and the essence of his consciousness. Whether Jesus truly existed or not, he is considered to be the personification of a consciousness that is entirely love-based. Despite the fact that such a consciousness cannot endorse the domination of the masculine over the feminine, this ideology has been used by the church since its inception. Imbalance, domination, and judgment stem from a lack of love. What religion is free from judgment and fear? This highlights the fact that religious dogma was established by men rather than by a divine consciousness. Most of the ideology built around the persona of Jesus fits into this category.

There are two types of people who are religious. The first type is childish; it is searching for a father figure. The first type is immature; it cannot rely upon itself, hence it needs a God somewhere or other. The God may exist or not—that is not the point—but a God is needed. Even if the God is not there, the immature mind will invent him, because the immature mind has a psychological need—it is not a question of truth whether God is there or not, it is a psychological need.

In the Bible it is said God made man in his own image, but the reverse is more true: man made God in his own image. Whatsoever is your need, you create that sort of God; that's why the concept of God goes on changing in every age. Every country has its own concept because every country has its own need. In fact, every single person has a different concept of God because his own needs are there and they have to be fulfilled.

So the first type of religious person—the so-called religious person—is simply immature. His religion is not religion, but psychology. And when religion is psychology it is just a dream, a wish fulfillment, a desire. It has nothing to do with reality.

Osho

From the Saga of False Gods to the Infiltration of the New Age Movement

Religious and New Age doctrines overlap and contradict each other at the same time. The overlapping is justified by the fact that they all tap into the underlying universal truth, or divine order. But where do the seeds of falsehood come from? The presence of concepts that contradict the mechanics of creation can be the result of a well-intentioned messenger who was contacted by the wrong entities and therefore channeled misaligned information, an ill-intended entity embodied as a messenger, or a manipulation of true knowledge for the purpose of misleading.

The virtue of New Age is that it liberates humans from the obligation of worshipping an external god; the movement owes its name to the introduction of this revolutionary paradigm. Another virtue of New Age is that it recognizes the existence of the secret anatomy and places the self at the core of personal healing, where mastery supersedes victimhood. The emphasis is on pursuing a personal path toward spiritual actualization instead of stifling self-expression in order to merge seamlessly with the socio-religious group.

The downside is that the body of knowledge collected by the New Age movement through channeling, contact, or cognition is not exempt from distortion. This represents a problem because the tools provided by New Age have a direct impact on the secret anatomy; misaligned codes, symbols, frequencies, activations, and brain entrainment can have devastating effects on the divine blueprint and can even initiate reversal mode. In order to avoid reversed ascension mechanics, DNA activation techniques, and frequencies (e.g. violet flame) from fallen disembodied collectives (e.g. Archangel Metatron and Michael), one can restrict oneself to mainstream self-improvement tools focused on acquiring mastery of thoughts and emotions.

Pragmatic Reality Constructs as Ersatz Religion and Spirituality

Alternative reality constructs to the religious paradigm are mostly the appanage of Western societies. They come in the form of philosophical currents like Cartesianism or positivism that dictate a certain cognition of reality. Pragmatic reality constructs also include the scientific paradigm, capitalism, hedonism, and consumerism, of which contemporary reality is a syncretism. These concepts mitigate the stronghold of the religious paradigm, allowing the modern construct of reality to be enriched with new perspectives. However, if the present paradigm is richer compared to the era of religious hegemony, it is still not exempt from distortion: instead of one convex mirror conveying an untrue image, there are now several.

Then there is the second type of religious people for whom religion is not coming out of fear. The first type of religion comes out of fear, the second type—also bogus, also pseudo, also so-called—is not out of fear, it is only out of cleverness. There are very clever people who go on inventing theories, who are very trained in logic, in metaphysics, in philosophy. They create a religion that is just an abstraction: a beautiful piece of artwork, of intelligence, of intellectuality, of philosophizing. But it never penetrates life, it never touches life anywhere; it simply remains an abstract conceptualization. When the third type comes in ... and that is the real type, these other two are the falsifications of religion, pseudo-dimensions—cheap, very easy, because they don't challenge you. The third is very difficult, arduous; it is a great challenge; it will create a turmoil in your life—because the third, the real religion, says God has to be addressed in a personal way.

Osho

Lost in Translation and the Educational System

The primary role of the educational system is to anchor the "official program." It is focused on grooming generations for the rat race rather than dispensing essential knowledge related to the mechanics of cocreation so that these are no longer called "The Secret." The requirements of the rat race, such as finding a job, paying the bills, and climbing up the social ladder, are so overwhelming that making a living becomes all there is to life. When one's energy units are focused on the rat race, there is hardly any time left for anything else; survival becomes the primary goal. What is the benefit of learning about wars fought by Napoleon when you are unaware of your secret anatomy and how it is constantly dictating your physical and spiritual destiny? The consequence is more and more generations lost in translation.

When I went to school, they asked me what I wanted to do when I grew up. I said: be happy. They told me that I hadn't understood the question. I replied that they hadn't understood life.

John Lennon

Social Constructs and the official program, or How People are Programmed to Sleepwalk through Life

The official program is a set of canned ideas at the core of time-defying value systems and reality constructs. It defines preconceived roles based on gender, normalizes the universal recipe for health and happiness, and provides an official meaning and purpose to life. Everybody is familiar with the preconceived roles related to gender—boys play with soldiers and don't wear pink or cry, and girls are expected to be interested primarily in cooking and breeding. The official program is very pedagogic so that nobody gets confused: the woman is the incubator while the man is the protector-provider. Failing to comply with the official program is sanctioned by blame and rejection on a social level, translating as feelings of guilt and shame on a personal level. The virtues of the official program are its normalizing and numbing effects. It provides a solid framework on a personal level and the appearance of order on a social level.

The official program as a reality construct is legitimized mainly through a manipulation of the right-wrong duality, and it is enforced by social punishment. A notorious example of a drastic social sanction is the chemical castration of Alan Turing in 1952 in punishment for his homosexuality. Although social punishment is no longer physical in modern societies, it is nonetheless effective, as it relies on fear-based tools to induce feelings of guilt and shame, which are the most toxic on Dr. Hawkins emotional scale. The primary tool of social punishment is judgment. Once the norm for what is right and wrong has been set within the framework of the official program, a clear line is then strongly established between the only reality that is allowed and what is referred to as digressive behavior that ought to be punished. The right/wrong duality can be manipulated so as to justify and legitimize fear-based consciousness like judgment, which qualifies as a behavioral distortion. It is a powerful and dangerous tool that has generated distorted value systems and legitimized throughout history the cruelest behavior.

The purpose of the official program is mainly twofold. It consists of creating a diversion while at the same time anchoring cognitive distortions that keep the divine blueprint misaligned and the contraction cycle blocked. The diversion it creates distracts us from the true purpose of our race, for which Mission Ascension is key. The objective is to program people to sleepwalk through life by giving them a set of officially recognized objectives and recycled aspirations to pursue.

Donkeys and Carrots

The universal recipe for happiness is the carrot that donkeys worldwide are pursuing. It is comparable to investing huge efforts in decorating a room on the Titanic. When remembrance of the human mission was lost, we couldn't be left down here purposeless. With the mutation and energetic harnessing of the human template came a distorted reality construct into which our mental and emotional bodies are now plugged. Just like the last thing a fish knows about is water, we are likewise unsuspecting of the matrix of fear-based morphogenetic fields that informs our reality, and we are unaware of its state of misalignment with the matrix of creation.

Chapter 7
Cognitive Distortions and Energetic Harnessing

The Matrix of Fear-Based Consciousness

Fear-based consciousness is an aggregate of mental viruses that create cognitive distortions, translating as an energetic prison. Imagine a road network where some streets get deviated, looping endlessly, while others get blocked. Similarly, mental distortions create dysfunctions and blockages that, though invisible to the naked eye, are as real as prison bars keeping us energetically harnessed. The official program as a by-product of a distorted reality construct is saturated with mental viruses, having each a corresponding fear-based morphogenetic field. We are trapped in a vicious circle where we are energizing the fear-based morphogenetic fields of shame, guilt, anger, etc., while being simultaneously affected by them through morphic resonance.

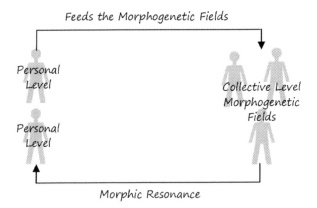

Feeds the Morphogenetic Fields

Personal Level

Personal Level

Collective Level Morphogenetic Fields

Morphic Resonance

The sum of individual subconscious minds forms the collective subconscious mind, which includes the fear-based morphogenetic fields that are fed by each person's shadow-self. If these are being more energized by individual thought-forms than the love-based morphogenetic fields, then morphic resonance is impacting us negatively. Should the love-based morphogenetic fields become more energized, morphic resonance will start impacting us positively.

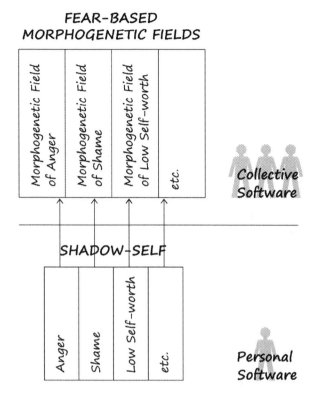

The misuse of the good/bad duality since early childhood inflates the shadow-self and consequently the fear-based morphogenetic fields. It embeds widespread toxic beliefs, such as "I am not good enough," "I have to do so many things in order to be loved and accepted," and "I need to compete and struggle," instead of "I am an expression of the divine," "Love and abundance are my birthrights," "I am here to play and cocreate," and "I can manifest with ease and grace." The toxicity of a negative program like "I am not good enough" justifies alone most of the fear-based behavior that sustains the dog-eat-dog world. Because it is embedded in most people, its morphogenetic field is so strong that it can be picked up on a psychic level, especially by children. So if you haven't inherited this transgenerational program, you are likely to pick it up through morphic resonance, given the magnitude of its morphogenetic field. Along with other mental viruses, it forms the backbone of the present paradigm, wherein individuals are imprinted with hundreds of fear-based programs, the most toxic one being that they need to do all sorts of things in order for them to be "enough" and to be accepted.

The fear-based collective software forms an intangible, but powerful matrix dictating human behavior, biasing it toward miscreation. This energetic prison compromises both spiritual and physical health. It represents an abnormality in the matrix of creation and generates distorted reality fields. Healing the collective software is first undertaken on an individual level until a critical mass is reached, beyond which the process becomes self-sustaining.

The Relationship between Cognitive Distortions and Energetic Harnessing

Because energetic harnessing relies mainly on miscreation, its objective is to mislead; this is where cognitive distortions step in. They have three main effects: 1) they are misleading, as they convey a deformed image of reality; 2) they therefore cause people to miscreate while they believe they are doing the right thing; and 3) because miscreation is fear-based, it is depleting and represents a powerful erosion tool by which energy is siphoned.

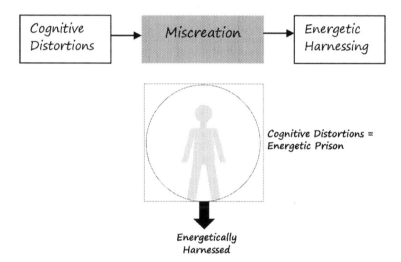

Cognitive distortions generated through the embedding of fear-based consciousness in the mental body are the tools by which energy is siphoned from the living matrix. This is why individuals who carry a certain load of mind viruses and calibrate under 200 Hz on Dr. Hawkins emotional scale are extremely depleted. When the mental body contains distorted concepts generally disguised as god-given values, both the spiritual and physical anatomies are damaged. The individual is in a state of constant depletion and misalignment with the matrix of creation, and therefore stuck on his evolutionary path. This is what energetic harnessing is all about: being stuck, mislead, disempowered, and preyed on.

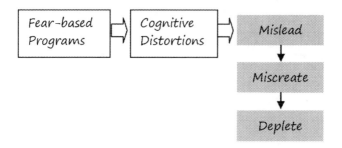

Quantum Draining

In an energetically harnessed system populated with depleted embodied and disembodied entities where quantum draining is constant, vampirism is the primary survival mode. It is how the parallel matrix drains energy from the matrix of creation and how energetically harnessed entities compensate for their constant state of depletion.

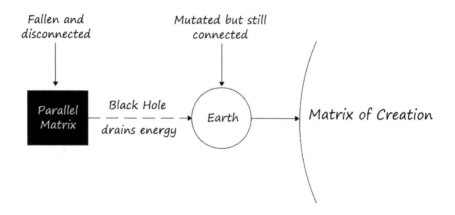

The fallen Milky Way is a closed system with two main characteristics: everything is subject to entropy and therefore in a constant state of depletion, and vampirism is the primary survival mode. Since the human race is in a state of energetic harnessing, everyone is likely to have unwanted cords with disembodied beings draining life force from them. Psychic hooks and cords also exist between embodied beings; they are formed between parents and offspring, siblings, friends, lovers, spouses, and coworkers. The victim/victimizer game is a default setting in most relationships. When somebody directs fear-based consciousness toward another, commonly referred to as a psychic attack, they are siphoning energy from that person. Conditional love, a by-product of the victim/victimizer mind virus is a distorted form of love, and yet the only one most of us will ever know.

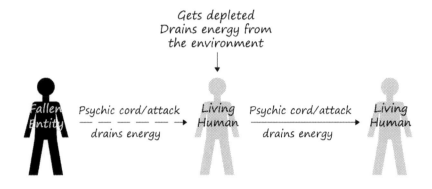

Gets depleted
Drains energy from
the environment

Fallen Entity — Psychic cord/attack — drains energy → Living Human — Psychic cord/attack — drains energy → Living Human

Quantum draining caused by endogenous factors like the shadow-self and the mutated human template, which blocks natural energy flow between an individuated consciousness and Source, is further aggravated by other exogenous factors.

ENDOGENOUS CAUSES OF DEPLETION

- Negative programming Shadow-self

- Mutated human template misaligned with the Divine Blueprint

EXOGENOUS CAUSES OF DEPLETION

- Vampirism
- Morphogenetic fields of fear-based consciousness
- Mind control tools: fear-based social constructs, biological, technological, etc.
- Unsacred geometry
- Negative abduction

Legitimate Forms of Vampirism

Social systems are pervaded with legitimate forms of vampirism. A lot of social values like "defending one's honor" are in reality fear-based concepts feeding the shadow-self. Similarly, neediness in a relationship is a form of vampirism disguised as love and faithfulness. Unconscious parenting is another common form of legitimate vampirism between genitors and their offspring, socially praised as raising the kids.

Vampirism is very strongly anchored in our reality construct, which explains the magnitude of the victim/victimizer program. If we imagined a world free from the victim/victimizer mind virus, we would be envisioning an entirely new paradigm. When we examine our relationships under this lens, we will realize that most of them are not exempted from this distortion. If one happens to experience a healthy relationship with his partner or spouse, then he probably plays the victim/victimizer game with his parents, siblings, friends, or coworkers. This distortion and its corollary, vampirism, are so widespread that saying they affect everyone is not an overstatement. The reason is that closed systems are vampire systems. Legitimizing vampirism in social constructs has proven its efficiency so far in sugarcoating the distortion, but the result is an endless recycling of the problem.

Chapter 7
The Other Aspects of Mind Control

The Tools of Mind Control

Mind control is key to energetic harnessing. It is multi-faceted and exerted on many levels, including mental, emotional and biological. It operates on the mental and emotional bodies namely by seeding fear-based concepts that generate an inaccurate cognition of oneself and the world and end up mutating the divine blueprint. It is exerted on a physical level through the use of biologically damaging tools, such as pharmaceutical drugs (e.g. Ritalin), home appliances like microwave ovens that mutate food, and industrial, public, and governmental facilities (e.g. HAARP). Since body and mind are closely interrelated, a damaged biology and DNA maintain and further aggravate distortions in the mental and emotional bodies and therefore facilitate mind control. Even food can be highly damaging, since toxins and extra weight block natural energy flow and curtail the accretion of consciousness and frequency.

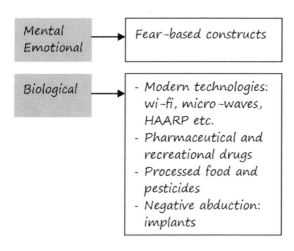

Biologically Damaging Tools

Because body and spirit are interrelated, biological damage prevents the human body from accreting consciousness and contributes to the ill health of the spiritual anatomy. The pharmaceutical and food industries are largely contributing to this process. Some medical drugs have been specifically conceived to alter and deactivate the DNA, for instance Ritalin, prescribed for children diagnosed with attention deficit disorder, or the infamous H1N1 vaccine. Other biologically damaging tools are modern technologies that rely on electromagnetic waves. Wireless connections and microwave ovens rely on low-frequency waves, whereas very high-frequency waves are used in governmental facilities like HAARP. Very low- and high-frequency waves can have adverse effects on the human biology and DNA; the overlapping and ubiquity of these waves forms a technological matrix with detrimental biological effects.

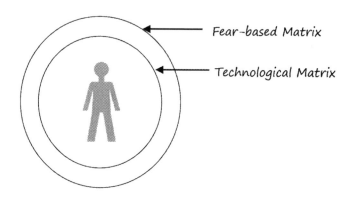

Fear-based Matrix

Technological Matrix

Unsacred Geometry

Signs and symbols as light patterns are not neutral. Unsacred geometry refers to a body of signs and symbols that anchor reversed frequencies and inorganic light (e.g. Fibonacci spiral). Some of these are religious signs, and a lot of famous shrines have been designed according to misaligned geometric shapes and volumes. Such signs are energized daily by millions of people through prayers and invocations. New Age has made a recent addition to unsacred geometry by channeling symbols that are misaligned with the mathematical/geometric code of the matrix of creation.

Negative Abduction

A recent poll has shown that 25 percent of Americans believe the reported negative abduction incidents to be true. Negative abduction is orchestrated by disembodied entities operating in reversal mode. We won't get into the technicalities of how this is achieved, but these incidents can occur astrally during sleep and don't necessarily involve a space ship landing in the backyard. Most victims remain forgetful of these incidents, even if they still carry the symptoms. For instance, many behavioral disorders, such as addictions, bipolar disorder, depression, and even suicide, are the result of negative abduction.

Chapter 8
Secret Wars

The Unknown Human Genome

The function of the human genome that has been elucidated by science so far does not include biological noncoding DNA, which accounts for more than 98 percent of our genes. Two characteristics of noncoding biological DNA can be outlined: 1) it proves the deactivation of our DNA evidenced by the fact that many coding sequences cannot braid together, and also by the presence of pseudogenes that are mutated and dysfunctional genes (of the genes that code the human olfactory system, more than 60 percent are pseudogenes, which explains why this sense is less developed in humans relatively to other mammals, especially dogs); and 2) it contains genes that are the biological expression of fear-based consciousness, like the endogenous retrovirus.

The not strictly human genes present in the yet-unknown nonbiological DNA template may also be expressed in noncoding biological DNA. Hybridization has been occurring all along the course of a long and uncharted human history, and a lot of negative abductions are driven by hybridization programs. An example of humans who carry the codes of fallen races are the Illuminati. Another example are the Indigo children, who carry the codes of races that are evolving in alignment with the matrix of creation and have therefore maintained the integrity of their divine blueprint. It is needless to say that these groups with their different codes are pursuing opposite agendas.

Secret Government and the Illuminati: Hoax or Reality?

The involvement of fallen entities in human affairs takes place through their middlemen, the Illuminati, a group of approximately 100,000 highly ranked individuals who form the secret government and international intelligentsia. The agenda of this group, known as the "dark agenda," can be broadly described as enabling the parallel system to sustain itself by harnessing our quanta. In a nutshell, fallen races are using us as their respirator, and one of their instruments is the secret government.

Some Illuminati have been tricked into collaborating with the fallen races by being promised new technologies, unsuspecting of what was really at stake. Such is the case of the Philadelphia experiment, where officials were tricked into believing they were given technologies to create an invisibility cloak around a military submarine so that it could go undetected by enemy forces. The experiment that took place to test these technologies was in reality creating a wormhole between our planet and the parallel matrix.

The role of the secret government is to feed the drama through wars and economic instability, and most importantly to maintain the oil-based economy. Although many governments have had contact with fallen entities since the early twentieth century, information related to alien contact has never been disclosed.

The Multifaceted Invisible War

The meddling of ill-intentioned disembodied races with human affairs, and the presence of their embodied representatives on earth, implies that a multifaceted secret war is happening right under our noses. The embedding of fear-based consciousness is the psychological war that has been taking place on the mental level for as far as anyone can remember. It consists of creating distortions in the mental body by anchoring fear-based programs. Our history of war, oppression, and injustice is proof of how deeply rooted fear-based consciousness is. As we have started very recently to escape from the stronghold of mental viruses and bring our construct of reality more into alignment with love-based consciousness, other secret wars have been initiated, like the chemical and frequency wars.

The aim of the chemical war is to damage our physical bodies and DNA through the engineering of harmful drugs, toxin-saturated foods, and even viruses. The frequency war consists of broadcasting harmful frequencies through earth grids, like the ones that are being emitted by HAARP and other broadcasting stations disguised as public facilities, urban landmarks, or even religious shrines. New Age groups contacted by ill-intentioned disembodied entities have also been anchoring the reversed frequencies of inorganic light (e.g. violet flame). All these combined efforts are not only aimed at keeping us energetically harnessed, but also at reaching a critical mass beyond which reversal mode is initiated on a mass level.

The reversed frequencies that earth has been subject to recently have been counteracted through the interference of Indigo groups striving to progressively anchor the frequencies of organic light. The presence of these groups with opposite agendas trying to anchor either organic or inorganic frequencies is the invisible frequency war.

Chapter 9
The Official Paradigm as a Distorted Construct

Successive Mutations: Loss of Abilities and State of Amnesia

It is hard to imagine that once upon a time humans were different from the race that we now know—that limitations, scarcity, struggle, ailment, aging, and death were not part of the agenda. Once upon a time, our planet was free from hospitals and cemeteries! Not only were limitations and decay not part of the picture, but also the human race was engineered with built-in abilities that we think only belong to the likes of Harry Potter.

Our race has incurred several mutations throughout the course of its history that spans far beyond the prehistoric era. These mutations are the result of miscreation and encounters with other races. Human DNA, which originally comprised twelve active strands, was progressively deactivated, leaving only a few strands operational. This explains the presence of biological and spiritual dysfunctions in the human template, our limited awareness that is comparable to a state of amnesia, and the loss of abilities that are now labeled as extrasensory and paranormal, the most important one being the ability to undergo biological ascension. Once upon a time, our race was able to embody more consciousness and remain aware of its multidimensional anatomy. The mechanics of creation and cocreation were common knowledge, and the mastery of thoughts and emotions was common practice.

Oblivion and Speculation: How Truth and Falsehood Permeate Everything

Oblivion is the mother of speculation. Philosophy and religion are the result of oblivion. They are both speculative theories about the origins and role of mankind in the universe. Science is taking baby steps toward understanding the mechanics of creation, including the nature of matter as energy, or consciousness. However, science is subject to linearity, thus requiring significant amounts of time to reveal simple facts. Science, religion, and philosophy are symptoms of the lost knowingness, attempts to recapture the forgotten truth.

What is the truth, anyway? When devoid of its poeticism and apprehended through logic, the concept of truth should define the divine order. In the human body, the fact that the liver is positioned to the right and the heart to the left represents the divine order of the human anatomy. Similarly, the anatomy of the universe obeys precise laws. How consciousness structures itself to create manifested and unmanifested realms can be defined as the truth, or divine order.

Let us use another analogy: to the human body, which is made of water, water is the truth, unlike any other fluid. Likewise, love-based consciousness is the substance of the divine blueprint. Whatever is not entirely love-based is therefore not entirely true. Because everything that exists in our closed system is made of a mixture of love and fear, we can ascertain that truth and falsehood permeate everything. This means that we have to play detective in order to discern truth from falsehood. Of course, it is much easier to absorb canned ideas and accept certain dogma as true; this is what most of us choose to do. It leaves plenty of free time to watch TV. Breaking free from collective illusions in search of the truth is the road less traveled.

Because truth and falsehood permeate everything, there is a thin line between them, and discernment is a muscle that can be built with practice. It is finding one's way out of a maze of misperceptions and illusionary reality fields. A misaligned concept can be easily interpreted as the truth, and conversely the truth can be disguised as falsehood, mocked, and discarded. This thin line between truth and falsehood is like the imperceptible one-degree angular shift that makes a ship end up in a completely different destination.

Earth as a Prison and a Hospital

Earth is a closed system where love- and fear-based consciousness, organic and inorganic light, are closely intertwined. Because fear-based consciousness and mind viruses permeate everything, it is not an overstatement to say that all forms of consciousness require healing, especially if they wish to exit our closed system and pursue their journey back to Source. The human template, burdened with inorganic components, acts like a straitjacket that doesn't allow anyone to go very far. Since healing is a prerequisite for all of us, it is also not an overstatement to say that earth is a universal hospital where individuals remain quarantined until they heal the fear-based and inorganic parts of their anatomy.

From this time forth, man may choose to no longer be enslaved by darkness; his destiny can then be certain.

Dr. David Hawkins

Preventing Mission Ascension is the "Stay Stuck so We Can Prey on You" Agenda

The fact that our planet is simultaneously connected to the parallel matrix and to the matrix of creation makes it an ideal harnessing field. This explains the unwavering interest of fallen races in us, as well as their constant meddling with human affairs. The existence of such entities is not compatible with our present reality construct, as it is very far from our mental conditioning with respect to what is real and what is not. Preventing Mission Ascension and harnessing earth's quanta is what entities operating in reversal mode are pursuing. This two-track secret agenda requires us to be mislead and disabled as a race, unable to break free from the energetic prison that we don't even know exists. Hence, energetic harnessing relies on spiritual, mental, emotional, and biological damage; it is the act of disrupting the divine order in order to siphon energy from the matrix of creation, like cracking a coconut to extract its milk.

Part III

The Hidden Science of Cocreation

Immerse yourself in the energy of what you desire.

Hiro Boga

Chapter 1

A Basic Step:
Healing the Shadow-Self

Why Healing Is the Primary Purpose of Life

The reason why healing should be a primary concern to everyone is that every individual living on earth is constrained by an energetic prison while having to deal with an array of other factors that are working against them. Everybody is born into a mutated template with inorganic components and is the victim of cognitive and behavioral distortions. This energetic prison is further reinforced by the matrix of fear-based consciousness and inorganic light, as well as mind control programs and covert manipulations by embodied and disembodied entities operating in reversal mode. Two consequences of the energetic prison are misperception and disempowerment; when we snap out of our false reality constructs, including the official program, and fathom what is really at stake, then healing is embraced as a way back to mastery and godhood.

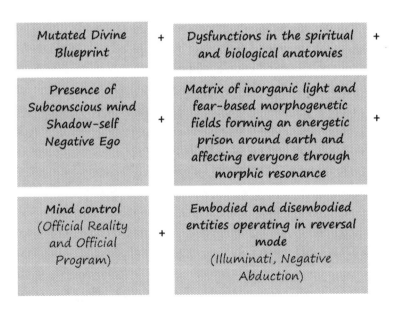

Understanding the Shadow-Self

Living on planet earth means having by default a shadow-self. Because our system is fear-based, this distortion affects everyone. If we compare ourselves to a house, then our shadow-self is the basement or attic that we hide behind the façade, where we dump all the unwanted stuff.

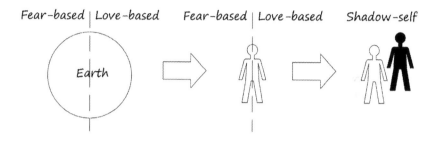

Fear-based consciousness stored in the subconscious mind forms the shadow-self. Healing the shadow-self is often referred to as healing the subconscious mind. Despite the fact that the shadow-self is an inorganic component, it has the virtue of storing unprocessed fear-based consciousness, thus buffering emotional pain. Its role is to conceal and delay, rather than to acknowledge, process, and resolve. Painful emotions never go away until they are identified and healed, so the shadow-self is a time bomb. Each time a fear-based incident takes place, it triggers negative emotions and beliefs that are automatically stored in the subconscious mind, especially if they are too painful to deal with and too emotionally overwhelming to process. Hence, the subconscious mind acts as a dumping ground for the junk that we don't know how to deal with because it is often too much for us to process.

The shadow-self is a default setting that we spend huge amounts of energy in trying to repress; this inorganic component is a permanent cause of quantum draining. Denial of the shadow-self is driven by feelings of shame and guilt that feed the negative ego. Thus, the presence of the negative ego is a reflection of a repressed shadow-self.

Fear-based consciousness ⟶ Shadow-self ⟶ Shame and Guilt ⟶ Negative Ego

Let us imagine the subconscious mind as a white dress, fear-based consciousness as stains, and life as a party where everyone is trying to make a good impression. Each person is spending huge amounts of energy trying to conceal the stains on the white dress, repressing and denying the shadow-self. The downside of this ongoing effort is that it is continuously draining huge amounts of energy and creating, through its corollary the negative ego, a string of cognitive and behavioral distortions. Healing the shadow-self is the act of removing the stains that are both transgenerational and accumulated throughout life. If the subconscious mind is the software dictating our physical reality and beyond, then these stains act like viruses corrupting the original program. They are different manifestations of the same cause, which is a lack of love. It is as if gasoline were spilled in the sea, contaminating every drop of water. It is now the responsibility of each drop to clean itself in order for the sea to be restored to its original condition.

Take a Look at Your Life

A practical way of exploring the contents of the shadow-self is to take a look at your own life, as situations and people mirror back to us different aspects of our own consciousness. Relationships, events, and life situations can all be used as pointers. If you want to know what lies in your subconscious, take a look at your life!

From this perspective, the limitations that one might be experiencing can be used as mirrors to uncover the underlying toxic programming. Instead of running away from limitations by shifting to denial mode, these can be used as doorways toward accessing the parts of our consciousness that require attention and healing. If a person is alone, despite the fact that he would like to be in a relationship, then that person is probably running one of the following programs:
- "I am not loveable."
- "I am not worthy."
- "My significant others always hurt me." ("If I let somebody get too close, I will get hurt.")
- "I will be abandoned."

If a person has an angry partner, or boss, then they are probably expressing what that person is repressing, and therefore mirroring to him what he is in denial of. Relationships and people are constantly reflecting to us different aspects of our consciousness, the ones that we express as well as the ones that we repress.

Your physical results don't lie.

Jack Canfield

Like Attracts Like

People who share the same programming and emotional frequency level find themselves evolving in the same bandwidths. Because like attracts like, the people around us are expressing or repressing qualities that we are either aware or unaware of. When we live our lives from a place of awareness, we can use the people around us as mirrors to unveil our subconscious programming. If you have an angry spouse, that usually means anger is one of your denied aspects of self. Both victim and victimizer are evolving in the same bandwidth, with one of them expressing what the other one is repressing.

The way out of an undesirable bandwidth is by acknowledging and healing hidden aspects of the shadow-self. Moving to a higher bandwidth will trigger a change in relationships and situations. When we shift our energy and frequency levels up significantly, the people around us will either evolve with us or no longer be part of our paradigm, and we will be attracting new friends, colleagues, bosses, partners, and lovers. Living from a place of awareness is knowing that life is constantly mirroring to us the invisible contents of our software.

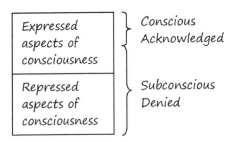

Repressed aspects of self are denied, whereas expressed aspects are either conscious or denied; even when a person expresses anger, he might be in denial of the fact that he reacted in an angry manner.

The Role of Self-Righteousness

Conscious fear-based behavior is justified by self-righteousness. When we hate someone, we always manage to find a justification: "I hate him because he is gay. Being gay is bad, and that gives me the right to resent him." If we pay close attention to the workings of the mind and to our inner dialogue, we will notice that each time we operate in fear mode, we manage to find justification for our behavior. Self-righteousness serves as a protective buffer for the shadow-self and negative ego.

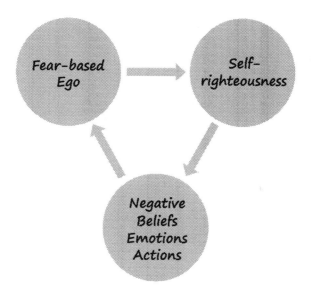

In order for the negative ego to stop dictating both cognition and behavior, the presence of the shadow-self must first be acknowledged. The role of self-righteousness is to conceal the shadow-self under the mask of rightful thinking. It acts as a ditch surrounding the fortress within which the shadow-self dwells; each time we are driven by the negative ego, self-righteousness steps in to justify the behavior by making us look good in our own eyes. It has succeeded so far in legitimizing the most unenlightened behavior and fear-based tenets disguised as God's will.

Racism and even acclaimed values like nationalism are expressions of self-righteousness. Healing the shadow-self requires deconstructing and unlearning many concepts disguised as "the right values." It is not an easy task, since entire value systems are based on self-righteousness; its role is to provide a makeup for fear-based consciousness.

Kinesiology as a Tool for Uncovering Subconscious Programming

Kinesiology is a technique commonly used to uncover the programming of the subconscious mind. It relies on muscle testing and is based on the principle that conflict between the conscious and subconscious minds weakens the body. This conflict occurs in the case of an untrue statement. To find out if you hold a certain subconscious belief, you can perform a muscle test. If your muscles weaken while you think a certain thought, it means the statement is untrue and that you do not hold that particular belief. One can muscle test for widespread beliefs like "life is a struggle" or "I need to struggle for money." One way to muscle test is to form a ring with the thumb and the index finger by making the tips of both fingers touch. A second person then tries to pull your fingers apart while you state that life is a struggle. If the fingers hold together, you do not have that particular belief. This simple method can help identify hundreds of beliefs held on a subconscious level that are orchestrating a person's life from behind his back.

Until you make the unconscious conscious, it will direct your life, and you will call it fate.

Carl Jung

Healing Techniques and Modalities

After uncovering a negative belief, the next step is to clear it. Simple do-it-yourself techniques can be used, such as positive affirmations. Caution is advised in seeking a healing modality; it is better to avoid ones that use colors, mantras, and symbols because the misuse of these elements can further aggravate distortions and even anchor the reversed frequencies of inorganic light. Techniques that stick to verbal reprogramming are safer because what you hear is what you get—there is no hidden risk.

An easy technique is to write down the opposite of a negative belief. If you think you are unlovable, then the opposite belief would be "I am lovable." Repeating the positive affirmation every day for a minimum of twenty-one days helps to create new neural pathways in the brain. Neuroscience has proven the elasticity of the brain, as well as the possibility of creating new cognitive patterns. The process can be further accelerated by adding conviction and emotion to the affirmation. Holding a thought with the positive emotion linked to it for more than seventeen seconds opens a new vortex through which more of this energy will flow into your paradigm. Opening and strengthening new vortices can be practiced every day.

Other do-it-yourself techniques include shifting to love-mode through monitoring one's intents and deeds. Doing random acts of kindness is a good way to initiate and amplify the process. The healing journey is a lifelong commitment, a daily hygienic practice like showering. It entails acquiring mastery of thoughts and emotions and moving up the emotional frequency scale through a sustained shift from fear to love-mode.

Taking Charge of Personal Energies

If we go back to the metaphor of oil spilling in a body of water, each polluted drop becomes responsible for its share of pollution and is faced with two choices, either to heal or to further contaminate others. Fear-based consciousness can be identified and healed or left unacknowledged, expressing itself through mind viruses and behavioral distortions, thus contaminating others and generating more of the same energy.

It is the responsibility of each individual not only to engage in the healing process, but also to direct his own energies. Taking charge of one's energy involves not only healing personal fear-based consciousness, but also managing it in order to minimize the impact of personal distortions on the environment. Each person's contribution to this twofold process is significant because of the principle of critical mass and morphic resonance. The more fear-based consciousness is transmuted on a personal level, the greater the healing effect that takes place on a collective level through morphic resonance. If you reach 300 Hz on Dr. Hawkins emotional scale, you may have a healing effect on a few people, but if you reach 700 Hz, you will impact thousands.

We may not be responsible for our inherited transgenerational fear-based programming and for the shadow-self that got formed in early childhood; nonetheless, we are now responsible for our own energy with its fear- and love-based components. It is our responsibility to manage and direct these energies, rather than to let ourselves be driven to miscreate and generate more of the same drama.

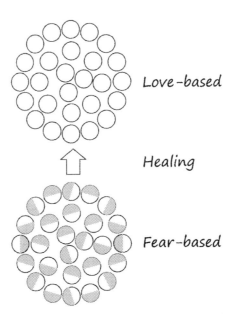

Love-based

Healing

Fear-based

Energy is always in motion, and so are our bodies, where trillions of cells die every day and are replaced by new ones. Through this process, the body is said to renew itself entirely in seven years or so, which means that it dies several times during its biological life span. We are constantly contributing to how the body transforms itself and evolves with time by the choices that we make and how we direct our energies in thought, emotion, and deed. Nothing is static—our physical hologram is like a car driving on a highway with us sitting in the driver's seat. Just imagine what would happen if the driver were not fully awake, aware, and able.

If we don't take responsibility for what we think and feel, others will make us feel and think in a certain way, which will cause us to create our own reality based on other's ideas, leading us to believe that we are at the mercy of a reality that exists apart from ourselves or that is 'thrust' upon ourselves.

There is no effect in our exterior world that does not spring from our own inner Source. We either create our own experiences or allow others to create them through us. Taking personal responsibility for, and realizing that at all times you are accountable for, directing personal energies is one of the Twelve Attitudes & Responsibilities of Mastery.

There is no one or no thing that 'upsets you'—you 'upset yourself' by allowing the emotional body to follow misperceptions of the mental body that tell you your power lies outside of yourself.

E'Asha Ashayana

Chapter 2
Welcome to the Contents of your Mind: Mindscapes Are Lifescapes

How Mental Distortions Create Distorted Reality Fields

Reality constructs are informed by cognition; in other words, they are mental constructs. What we are unsuspecting of is the extent to which these constructs are pervaded with misaligned concepts that translate as mental distortions. Let us examine something very commonly practiced, like worship. What if the need to worship something or someone were a behavioral distortion affecting the mental and emotional bodies? Not only is this distortion institutionalized, but also people who display external signs of worship are more likely to earn their peers' respect. The need to worship is mainly driven by our current state of unknowingness, which breeds disempowerment. The concept of worship forms a fear-based morphogenetic field acting like a powerful energetic net, in which most people are ensnared. Entrapment in this misperception entails maintaining a state of mental and emotional immaturity, whereas the whole purpose of any spiritual quest is the return to godhood.

This is only one example of the many distorted reality fields in which we may be ensnared. Not feeling worthy is another mental distortion that generates the reality field of victimhood. Other distorted constructs include the need to feel superior to others, which translates as racism, nationalism, the need to label and judge, the rat race, etc. So many of these distorted reality fields based on misperception pervade and inform the construct that we call reality and form benchmarks that define the norm.

The Universal "Groundhog Day"

Distortions of the mental body inform both the physical and nonphysical realms. Hence, the key role of the mind extends beyond resolving life's issues and healing recurrent negative patterns—it is the control center of one's holographic reality, whether in embodied or disembodied form. In other words, the key role played by the mental body stretches beyond physical death, as the hologram that persists on a nonphysical plane is subject to the same mental distortions held when in physical form. These distortions translate as mutations in the divine blueprint that impede an individuated consciousness from resuming its journey back to Source. This unnatural situation has given birth to a process called reincarnation.

Because an individuated consciousness with a distorted mental body cannot undertake the contraction cycle, it has no other choice than to reincarnate. When it does, it inherits the distortions of its biological family and plugs into the fear-based morphogenetic fields surrounding earth. If it doesn't initiate the healing process, it will undergo physical death with the same distortions in a reduced or aggravated form and will therefore reincarnate again. It is an endless cycle of birth and death, a universal Groundhog Day; this recycling wheel is known as the wheel of karma from which Buddhists are so desperately trying to break free. The exit from the recycling wheel is through healing the mental body, which then restores the emotional body and the rest of the divine blueprint. It does not require retiring to a remote monastery; it is a process that can be undertaken from one's own living room.

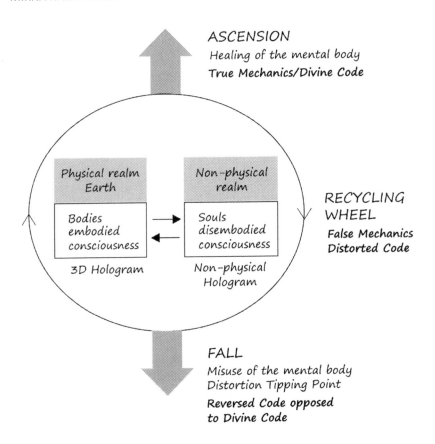

ASCENSION
Healing of the mental body
True Mechanics/Divine Code

Physical realm
Earth

Bodies
embodied
consciousness

3D Hologram

Non-physical
realm

Souls
disembodied
consciousness

Non-physical
Hologram

RECYCLING
WHEEL
**False Mechanics
Distorted Code**

FALL
Misuse of the mental body
Distortion Tipping Point
**Reversed Code opposed
to Divine Code**

Negative Programming

The contents of the mind are the storyboard of reality, largely informed by negative programming stored on an individual and collective level, respectively, in the mind and the collective subconscious. If one does not receive a certain program as part of his transgenerational makeup, he is very likely to pick it up on a psychic level through morphic resonance. Therefore, widespread mind viruses that have reached a critical mass form a net in which people are ensnared by default, like for instance low self-worth. This issue is linked to one's ability to achieve financial success, which explains why wealth is concentrated in the hands of only five percent of the world population. The relationship between achieving financial wealth and self-worth illustrates the magnitude of mind viruses and their stronghold on both cognition and behavior.

The dog-eat-dog world is a by-product of another widespread core belief, "I am not good enough," that generates a behavioral distortion like the need to compete for love. This toxic belief is a default setting, the result of unconscious parenting, social systems based on competition and judgment, and morphic resonance. Being unlovable represents the ultimate fear. This explains the efficiency of social pressure, as individuals are afraid of losing the "love" and acceptance of the social group to which they belong. This process has successfully maintained social customs in place for thousands of years, along with the cognitive distortions that are inherent to them.

TRUTH Divine Blueprint	MIND VIRUS Cognitive Distortion	BEHAVIORAL DISTORTION	REALITY CONSTRUCT
I AM WORTHY I AM LOVEABLE	I AM NOT GOOD ENOUGH I AM UNLOVEABLE	I NEED TO COMPETE FOR LOVE	DOG-EAT-DOG WORLD

We all start our earthly journey from the wrong premise that we are not good enough—i.e. unlovable—and we spend huge amounts of energy doing two things: 1) suppressing the negative feeling of not being good enough and 2) competing with others and looking for love in all the wrong places by listening to our negative ego. Our default settings are working against us and putting us off track. The unconscious and conscious fear of losing love is the main informant of human behavior and results in collective behavioral distortions, such as the need to compete for love, material possessions, parental and social approval. Reality constructs built on these misperceptions are energy-draining and not conducive to spiritual actualization. Healing reality is the process of healing the mind that creates and endorses it.

Fear and Reversal Mode

Negative programming is the main driver of miscreation. When they both cross a tipping point in a person, he starts operating in reversal mode, in which more than half of his beliefs, thoughts, emotions, and actions are fear-based. Reversal mode is when the conscious mind wishes for something positive, but the subconscious mind is so soaked up in negativity that it simply doesn't allow it to happen. Unfortunately, the subconscious wins because it represents more than 99 percent of the mind.

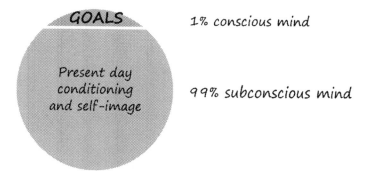

1% conscious mind

99% subconscious mind

Goals are generally love-based desires, but if more than half of one's thoughts and emotions are fear-based, then most likely the subconscious mind will not allow them to manifest. Being burdened with a fear-based subconscious mind is like wearing weights around your ankles while trying to run a marathon. Pursuing goals is generally a good excuse for initiating the healing process of the mind. The desire to achieve positive physical results acts as a driver for reversing negative programming.

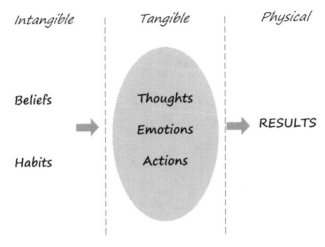

Figure 10. Key informants of physical results (Source: John Assaraf)

Years ago, when brain science was in its infancy, a test was done on a Northern Pike ... a common freshwater predator in the northern hemisphere. Scientists put it in one side of an aquarium with a glass divider, and filled the other side with minnows. The hungry pike immediately went after the minnows, banging his nose against the glass.

This went on for some time, until eventually the pike gave up. He learned his lesson. That's when it got interesting: the scientists removed the glass divider! The minnows swam all around him, but it didn't matter to the pike.

He had been conditioned that whenever he tried to go after the minnows, he'd hurt his nose. They could swim right through his open mouth, and he wouldn't even try. The 'Pike Syndrome' was one of the earliest tests that demonstrated how our conditioned thoughts, beliefs, and habits can cripple us, hold us back, cause uncertainty, doubts, fears, anxieties, and so much more. And how we ourselves can retrain our brains in ways that hold us back or make us successful.

John Assaraf

Acquiring Mastery of Thoughts and Emotions

Mastery of thoughts and emotions is the primary tool for restoring the imprint for health. Converse to what we commonly believe, physical reality is only holographic, whereas our mental and emotional bodies are the real substance behind the script that we call life. Thoughts and emotions are navigation and cocreation tools. Knowledge of these tools is a requisite for cocreation, while ignorance of them is the root of miscreation.

Whether we are working with them consciously or not, thoughts and emotions are continuously informing our multilevel anatomy and reality. Despite the fact that mastery of thoughts and emotions is the cocreation tool *par excellence*, this basic knowledge was only shared by a small elite and transmitted within secret societies and mystery schools until it was brought to the masses on an unprecedented scale by the author Rhonda Byrne. She rightfully named it "The Secret" because it has been willingly kept from the masses, in order to keep them in victimhood mode. The result of this ignorance is that instead of controlling our thoughts and emotions in a way that serves our highest purpose, we are controlled by them in detrimental ways. Awareness of the key role played by thoughts and emotions is essential in order to upgrade from passivity to captainship. These tools are not yet part of mainstream culture, despite the success of the self-help industry, because we only tend to take seriously information that is dispensed through institutional systems.

The smart management of thoughts and emotions is an essential stepping-stone out of victimhood toward godhood. It starts with the basic exercise of monitoring one's thoughts and emotions, exactly like looking for weeds in a garden. Because our consciousness is initially entirely love-based, anything that is biased toward fear is denaturing.

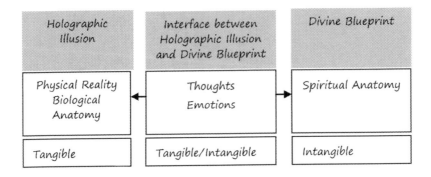

Because like attracts like, negative thoughts and emotions attract matching physical events that trigger more of the same energy. This vicious circle has a tipping point, or negativity threshold, beyond which an individual starts operating in reversal mode. The opposite is also true; a positivity threshold can be reached, beyond which love-based thoughts, emotions, and actions supersede fear-based consciousness. To operate in love-mode allows for a progressive restoration of the divine blueprint and the recovery of former built-in abilities like swift manifestation.

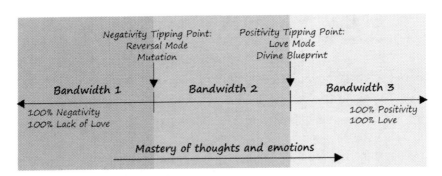

The presence of the negativity and positivity tipping points determines three bandwidths:

Bandwidth 1 corresponds to reversal mode and is characterized by a mutation of the divine blueprint and a disconnection from Source, which results in a progressive depletion. Vampirism is the main characteristic of this bandwidth.

Bandwidth 2 is located between the negativity and positivity tipping points, where most people who haven't yet achieved mastery of thoughts and emotions are likely to find themselves.

Bandwidth 3 is where love-based consciousness supersedes negativity. This path of realignment with the matrix of creation restores the imprint for health, and with it the potential for ascension beyond our closed system.

Law of Attraction: The Manifesting Machines and the Lost Instruction Manual

Energy is always in motion; it is constantly being transmuted into either fear- or love-based consciousness. The process can be intentional or unintentional; its instruments are thoughts and emotions that translate as actions. The mechanism of the law of transmutation, a sub-law of the law of attraction, is extremely simple: whatever we bring our consciousness to and channel energy toward will be transmuted from the invisible world of possibilities to our physical world. Nothing is real until it is observed. Observing is bringing consciousness to something, channeling energy toward it. This explains why the law of attraction is a physical law like the law of gravity. Since we are always directing our consciousness toward things, we are therefore constantly attracting these things into our lives. This process runs on automatic pilot; just like the metabolism, it is constantly engaged in sophisticated workings that we are unaware of.

Our cluelessness about the mechanics of manifestation and cocreation has turned us into deficient manifesting machines operating without an instruction manual. This explains why we are surrounded by things that we don't want, and why our daily routine includes complaining about almost everything. It is not that we live in a perfect world where there is nothing to complain about; it's just that by being passive whiners, we will neither change the way things are, nor extract ourselves from the looping system that we find ourselves in. Whether we are in an ideal setting or in a less-than-perfect one, the only attitude possible is that of being a proactive fixer of things rather than a passive victim.

Because the law of attraction is a physical law like the law of gravity, we are constantly attracting relationships and events into our lives by producing thoughts and emotions based on our belief system. What we are attracting is a match to what we are thinking and feeling because the law of attraction is indiscriminating, like the law of gravity. If a car goes off a cliff with a baby inside it, the law of gravity won't say, "I'll just take the car and spare the innocent baby," because it is indiscriminating. The same applies to the law of attraction. If a person is engaged in a vicious circle of toxic patterns yielding more and more negative results, the law of attraction won't say, "Oh, poor guy! He's had enough trouble already," because it is indiscriminating. Just like the law of gravity, it is a physical law. The advantage of reaping what we sow is that it allows us to be fully responsible for our life and results.

Because what we observe will become real, we might as well start becoming aware of these very powerful laws—the law of transmutation and the law of attraction—by getting them to work for us. In other words, it is better to learn how to use matches in order not to burn your fingers. We are unlikely to win any game if we don't know the rules. Energy is neither created nor lost—it is only transformed. It is constantly in motion and flowing somewhere: it can be consciously harnessed and channeled toward cocreation or left to flow in all the wrong directions. Channeled energy is like a powerful stream, whereas unchanneled energy is like a flood. The law of transmutation is working in our lives on a permanent basis because we are constantly transmuting consciousness, whether we are aware of it or not. From this perspective, each minute that passes by brings with it the opportunity to start turning things around by getting the laws to work for us, not against us.

If You Wish for a Million Dollars, Don't Be Surprised If It Doesn't Fall on Your Lap!

If you wish for a million dollars, don't be surprised if it doesn't fall on your lap. As T. Harv Eker said, "Success comes from fullness, not from lack." It is not just about the results, but also about the process. Results are only one component of the equation.

Process + Change = Results

One cannot expect results without going through the process and the change. Results like earning a million dollars are a destination that is chosen, but a journey needs to be made in order to get there. It is all about the journey, the end result is something that you reap as a reward for your undertaking. So if you set one million dollars as your destination and commit to taking the journey from lack to fullness by shifting to love-mode, then the money will be yours. It will come as a reward, or a physical proof of the positive changes that have been made. Every investment made in positivity yields a positive physical return. So when you reach your destination, the real achievement is not the physical reward, but who you have become in order to achieve it.

What if what I am learning in the meantime is even better than the "it" happening now?

Paul Bauer

Fake It Until You Make It, or the Benefits of Future Causation

"We get what we are and not what we want, because being is the first cause of everything." This quote from Harrison Klein means that it is not enough to want; you must become. If you know you must end procrastination, that doesn't mean that you will stop procrastinating. Therefore, wanting is not enough. It is only the trigger, the key that unlocks the door. Only becoming will allow the door to swing open and for new dimensions and states of being to be accessed. It is all in the being, hence Socrates' infamous quote "Become who you are."

What separates the future self from the present one is frequency rather than time; the future self does not exist in a distant time, but in a different bandwidth. The envisioned future self is an empowered probable self, and what the present self can do is step into that power.

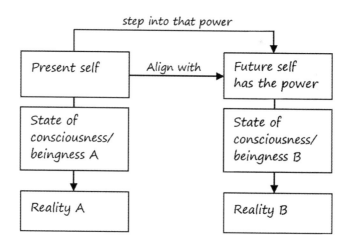

Future causation can be used to achieve desired states of being. It is the process of actualizing the future self by drawing upon its mental, emotional, and energetic properties. The idea is to birth into the now an ideal or future self by progressively embodying its mental and emotional states. This simple exercise has the virtue of changing one's energy signature, thus birthing the ideal self into physical reality. Future causation is commonly referred to as "fake it until you make it." If your ideal self is wealthy, how would your relationship be with money? It is very unlikely that you would be continuously afraid of running out of it, or that you would doubt your ability to generate it or even be burdened with a scarcity mentality. It is hard for someone on minimum wage to embody all at once the mental and emotional states of a wealthy future self; however, incremental changes can be made toward the desired goal. Healthy desire is a calling of the soul toward evolution and perfection. So when you close your eyes and envision an ideal self, no matter how remote this vision may seem from your present reality, it is always worth taking the journey toward that future self. What starts incrementally finishes off exponentially, as one builds momentum through commitment and perseverance. In the confrontation between water and rock, water wins through perseverance.

The law of attraction is this: You don't attract what you want. You attract what you are.

Dr Wayne Dyer

Building the Ideal Self Energetically

Each person has many probable selves, depending on how he is directing consciousness and on the paths that he continuously chooses. The ideal self represents the best probable self that can be achieved in a single lifetime. Because it is envisioned by the mind, the ideal self meshes spiritual actualization with a certain degree of cognitive distortion, depending on how mentally and emotionally mature the person is. Nonetheless, it is worth pursuing the ideal self for two main reasons: 1) acting out the mental and emotional distortions and reaching more spiritual maturity, and 2) achieving spiritual actualization. If one's ideal self is endowed with fortune and fame, then achieving this ideal self will help to act out this desire and replace it with more spiritually mature goals.

An ideal future self represents a self that has accreted more consciousness and frequency. Its qualities can be actualized in the now—it is the process of engineering the energetic blueprint of the ideal self and of getting in sync with one's true purpose and deepest longings. Desire, or the true longing of the soul, is not to be confused with mundane cravings like coveting a pair of expensive shoes. Connecting with the ideal self, with the inner vision, allows one to get progressively in sync with its qualities and purpose. These may seem daunting and unrealistic as compared to the self situated in the now. Nonetheless, the ideal self can be set as a cherished destination toward which one can start taking the journey energetically. There is no need to worry about the how, it will take care of itself. The important thing is to remain focused on building that new energetic blueprint.

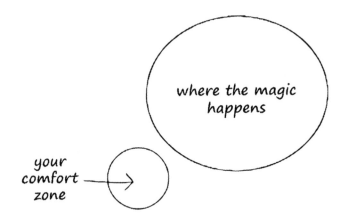

The Heroic Probable Self

A probable self is birthed by directing consciousness in a certain direction. Of all the probable selves, the heroic probable self is the one that corresponds to the ideal self as envisioned by a distortion-free mind. Whatever can be envisioned exists and can therefore be actualized. Focusing on heroic probabilities is the act of pursuing an integral realignment with love-based consciousness through every deed and state of being.

Each individual has a heroic probable self waiting to be actualized, but it is currently overridden by the three-dimensional identity. The earthly personality is informed by transgenerational, parental, and social fear-based consciousness in addition to personal karma. It is therefore conditioned by the shadow-self. When perception is confined to the physical arena and self-awareness is restricted to the earthly identity, the heroic self remains unexpressed. Birthing this probability into the now requires freeing the heroic self from its energetic prison formed by the distortions of the earthly identity.

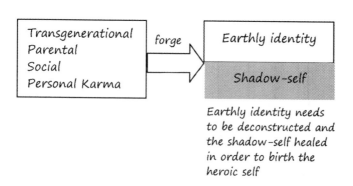

Earthly identity needs to be deconstructed and the shadow-self healed in order to birth the heroic self

Lifescapes are Mindscapes: The Power of Now

Reality as a projection of the contents of the mind has a holographic nature, of which time and space are two components. We tend to think that thoughts, because of their intangible nature, are less real than what we see. The opposite is true, since physical reality is only a holographic projection of the unseen contents of the mind. Understanding how things really work is essential in order to reclaim control over our reality field: since it is generated in the mind, whatever is not desirable can be undone and its opposite created.

The past and the future as components of holographic reality are as illusionary as time and space. The simultaneity of past, future, space, and time is hard to fathom by a mind cognitively locked into the linearity of three-dimensional reality. The illusion of linearity allows for physical reality to be experienced the way it is, just like the law of gravity allows for life to unfold on the back of our planet. Although essential to our physical dimension, linearity and gravity are not universal, since they don't apply in other parts of the cosmos. Understanding the illusionary nature of linearity is the doorway to undoing the past and tailoring the future. The present moment is the point of power from which this is achieved.

The mental body is the script upon which physical reality is based, as well as the place where fear-based consciousness and the past are stored. The now is the portal through which this control center can be accessed. The mental body with its fear-based components is like an internal garden ravaged by weeds, the clearing of which can only take place in the present moment. Each time a sustained positive thought overrides a negative core belief, the past is progressively undone. Directing thoughts and creating new realities takes place in the now through conscious acts of free will.

NOW	+	Directing consciousness/ thoughts	=	Changing the contents of the mind	+	Recreating the past Creating the future

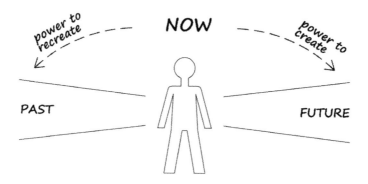

Working with the mental body to mold the future is just as simple, once we understand that reality is produced by actualizing desired states of being; it is the embodiment in the present moment of a desired mental and emotional state that causes it to manifest. If the mental body is the software that codes reality, the now is the portal through which the mental body can be accessed and reprogrammed. The present is the point of power where we become masters of our own illusion; each moment can be harnessed to regain control of the mental body and, concomitantly, physical reality.

If you correct your mind, the rest of your life will fall into place.

Lao Tzu

You are always free to change your mind and choose a different future, or a different past.

Richard Bach

Chapter 3
Moving Up the Emotional Frequency Scale

Energy Signatures: Consciousness Translates as Frequency

Each person is constantly emitting different types of frequencies. When you have an argument, you are emitting a type of frequency different from the one you would be emitting if you were meditating, or feeling joy. These frequencies, which are being emitted constantly, impact the environment, including people and morphogenetic fields. However, they affect first and foremost the person who is emitting them. They leave a footprint on the mental, emotional, etheric, and physical bodies, as well as other components of the secret anatomy like the geometric template, the cycle of fission-fusion, and the ARPS, thus altering the frequency level. Consciousness translates as frequency: the corollary of fear-based consciousness is low frequency because this type of consciousness causes the cycle of fission-fusion to slow down. Conversely, a high frequency level is the characteristic of love-based consciousness.

100% fear-based   *100% love-based*

200 Hz   500 Hz

Controlled by Shadow-self
Operates in Reversal Mode
Service to Self
Vampirism

Disengagement from Shadow-self
Operates in Love Mode
Oneness
Return to Godhood

No two people or pebbles are alike, and the same applies to energy signatures. These can be grouped within bandwidths that correspond to frequency ranges. As previously discussed, the bandwidth situated below 200 Hz on Dr. Hawkins emotional frequency scale can be referred to as the reversal mode bandwidth. Its main characteristics are fear-based consciousness and a powerful shadow-self dominating the personality. The consequence is the inability to draw energy from Source because of a strong state of misalignment; therefore, drawing energy from the environment becomes the only remedy for depletion. The bandwidth above 500 Hz is where love-based consciousness overrides fear-based consciousness. It is the doorway to sustainable healing, higher awareness, and empowerment, and a stepping stone to godhood.

Bandwidth below 200 Hz	Bandwidth beyond 500 Hz
- Fear-based consciousness - Misalignment with Source - Inability to draw energy from Source remedied for by vampirism - Personality dominated by shadow-self - Victimhood and scarcity mentality - Mutation of the Divine Blueprint - Inability to manifest - Inability to ascend, endless reincarnation cycle	- Love-based consciousness - Alignment with Source - Draws energy from Source, ability to replenish oneself - Personality synchronized with higher-self - Mastery of thoughts and emotions - Healing of the Divine Blueprint - Ability to manifest - Ability to ascend

Moving through Bandwidths

An emotional frequency bandwidth is determined by a set of parameters that include the percentage of fear- and love-based consciousness, organic and inorganic light, the state of emotional and mental health, the frequency level, etc. To each emotional frequency bandwidth can be matched a mental state and an energy signature, translating as a certain physical reality. The bandwidth situated below 200 Hz is characterized by a mental state with its matching array of beliefs where victimhood, struggle, and scarcity prevail. In this bandwidth, the core belief is that life happens to us; therefore, individuals who calibrate under 200 Hz are busy either blaming or complaining. They are trapped inside the victim/victimizer illusion. When they blame, they are victimizers; when they complain, they are victims. The victim/victimizer paradigm represents a major distortion of the mental body. Freedom from this distortion takes place when one reaches the level of 500 Hz and beyond.

Calibrating under 500 Hz usually means that thoughts and emotions are not being directed in a constructive manner; it also denotes a significant presence of inorganic light compromising the divine blueprint. Bandwidths situated below 500 Hz are the "hamster on a wheel" reality fields where many limitations are experienced. Vampirism is another characteristic of these bandwidths, since low emotional frequency entails depletion. Beyond 500 Hz, the paradigm of victimhood, passivity, and miscreation is replaced by mastery, responsibility, and cocreation. A person at this level contributes to the healing of others through morphic resonance. A leap from one bandwidth to the other is accompanied by changes in the physical arena, as one finds himself playing a different game with new players. Because like attracts like, events and people matching the new energy signature will be attracted into one's paradigm.

If you wish to understand the Universe, think of energy, frequency and vibration.

Nikola Tesla

How Emotional Blocks Work

Emotional blocks are filters that prevent emotions of a higher frequency level to be fully experienced and their matching reality fields to manifest. If someone has been humiliated to a traumatic extent, so as to form an emotional block, then he will not allow into his life events or people that will generate emotions of a higher frequency level than shame. Such a person will appear to be stuck in a rut; no matter how much effort he puts in, he is still not able to move to a higher bandwidth. Heavy emotional blocks caused by severe trauma act literally as concrete walls between an individual and self-actualization. If one is born into a bandwidth that we will refer to as baseline bandwidth, unprocessed heavy emotional blocks will cause a lifelong imprisonment within that same bandwidth.

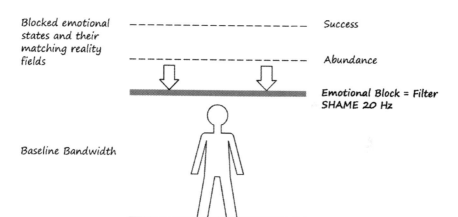

Blocked emotional states and their matching reality fields

Success

Abundance

Emotional Block = Filter
SHAME 20 Hz

Baseline Bandwidth

Moving Out of Victimhood

Mastery and victimhood don't match because one is either a victim or a master. Moving out of victimhood is a prerequisite for taking charge of one's life and the foundation upon which mastery is progressively built. Victimhood is acted out in the form of two roles, that of victim and victimizer. Although they appear to be contradictory, these two roles belong to the same bandwidth because one of them is expressing what the other one is repressing. They both denote the presence of a high percentage of fear-based consciousness. Therefore, the victim/victimizer drama cannot be resolved transversally; it can only be outgrown by moving, through mental and emotional healing, beyond the bandwidth of victimhood.

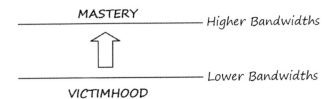

In the victimhood bandwidths, the attitude is more of taking, and not much creative energy is generated. Conversely, in the mastery bandwidths, the attitude is more of giving and contribution to society, and mankind is greater. Outgrowing the victim/victimizer game means stepping outside the old paradigm where people are conditioned to see themselves as disempowered by default. Victimhood is institutionalized, namely by religion, which depicts us as sinners who have to woo a judgmental god for redemption. This distortion also extends to the parental context, where children are treated as disempowered creatures that have to continuously please their genitors in order to win their acceptance. Moving out of victimhood implies a cultural change because this mentality permeates our present paradigm as an intrinsic component of reality.

The Blame Game and Ho'oponopono

The victim/victimizer distortion is accompanied by three mind viruses: judgment, blame, and punishment. The material found on newsstands and television feeding the social and political drama relies on judgment, blame, and punishment. Almost everyone is ensnared in these powerful morphogenetic fields, and a significant proportion of the 60,000 thoughts that the human mind is said to produce daily is dedicated to judging and blaming.

Victim/victimizer

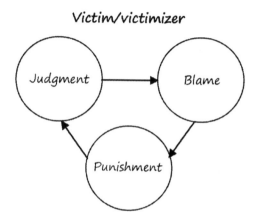

Freedom from the victim/victimizer bandwidth starts by disengaging from blame and replacing it with awareness and emotional healing. Techniques like *ho'oponopono* can be used to tackle blame experienced by both the victim and victimizer. It consists of the following mantra that can be repeated whenever the urge to blame is felt: "I apologize. Please forgive me. Thank you. I love you." Because words are codes, the encryption of the *ho'oponopono* mantra can be used to override the reversed frequency of blame. It may seem far-fetched to apologize mentally to someone who we think is to blame. When we are operating in fear mode, the mind will always trick us into believing that we are right to react in a certain way. The idea is to quiet the voice of self-righteousness that can be extremely misleading and to engage the *ho'oponopono* process. Adding emotion and conviction to the mantra is important. When mentally apologizing to a person who we think is to blame, we can ask ourselves what this situation is teaching us and what hidden aspects of our shadow-self it is mirroring to us. Blame is what we usually resort to when a hidden aspect of the shadow-self is making us emotionally uncomfortable. Like overeating and other addictions, it is a quick fix used to deal with repressed emotions. Very often, a deteriorated self-image, held on a subconscious level, is creating the victimhood situation and generating the need to blame.

Frequency Bandwidths and the 3S: Self-Respect, Self-Image, and Self-Actualization

Self-image as part of the mental landscape plays an essential role in emotional healing, and it is a key informant of holographic programming and physical reality. Many areas that need improvement in one's hologram can be linked to issues of self-image. Self-respect is the backbone of a healthy self-image, and the lack of it will always translate as negative life situations. In the case of a homeless person, the economic situation is not the only thing to blame; the individual is running a program from which self-respect is completely absent, and therefore his self-image will never allow him to attract and enjoy abundance. Even if a woman meets an attractive man, if her self-image is running a negative program like "I am unsexy and unlovable," she will not be able to fully experience her sensuality and will eventually sabotage the relationship.

Healing the self-image is an essential step toward improving holographic reality; you will never have what your self-image will not allow you to. Tangible results like money, toys, relationships, and even how our physical bodies evolve with time are all crafted by the conscious and subconscious self-image held within the mind. Mending self-images is usually an incremental process, like climbing stairs. There is a time lag between each improvement made on the mental level and the unfolding of physical events matching the new self-image. After sustained improvement has been made, positive change becomes exponential as one capitalizes on the previous efforts and is rewarded by positive life situations that will further reinforce his new self-image.

Self-images are multifaceted and comprise conscious and subconscious layers. Dealing with the subconscious self-image is tricky because it represents the larger, hidden part of the iceberg. You may be conscious of some aspects of your self-image, if you don't like your body, for example, but there are many subconscious aspects that people are unaware

MIRNA HANNA Ph.D.

of—for instance, a lack of self-respect. This subconscious program is the result of negative beliefs about one's worthiness, formed mainly during childhood. Someone who is disrespected as a child will form a self-image from which self-respect is absent. A self-image without self-respect is like a body without a spinal cord. Unfortunately, disrespect is common practice in relationships between adults and children and is often disguised as legitimate adult authority. This mental virus is responsible for unhealthy self-images, dysfunctional behavior feeding the victim/victimizer game, and negative life situations characterized by lack and limitations.

etc.	More self-actualization
Frequency Bandwidth n+2	Improved relationships including relationship with self
Frequency Bandwidth n+1	
Baseline Frequency Bandwidth n	Improved self-image and self-respect

Restored self-respect and self-image are prerequisites for achieving self-actualization, just like two healthy legs are required to run a marathon. Not only do a damaged self-respect and self-image act as roadblocks as one is trying to achieve self-actualization, but they also translate physically as the "life is a struggle" bandwidths. Restoring these two pillars of manifestation requires, namely, the identification and healing of major emotional blocks, including low self-worth issues.

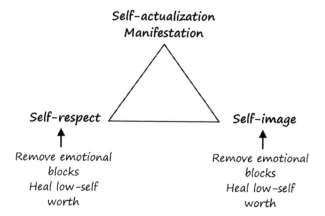

Self-actualization
Manifestation

Self-respect

Self-image

Remove emotional
blocks
Heal low-self
worth

Remove emotional
blocks
Heal low-self
worth

The Effect of Low Self-Worth

Low self-worth is a widespread core encryption simultaneously fed by transgenerational, parental, and social sources in addition to inner dialogue and morphic resonance. Low self-worth generates a wobbly self-image, where one envisions himself as a victim. This translates physically as being part of the working class, as opposed to the creative class; the energetic harness is much stronger in this bandwidth, where life is experienced primarily as a struggle with a string of limitations.

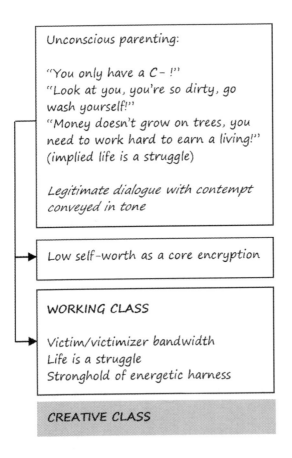

Low self-worth is often seeded by legitimate dialogue, in which the conscious or unconscious desire to belittle is conveyed in the tone rather than in the statement itself. Hence, most covertly undermining statements are not considered as abusive and are common practice in the parental and social contexts.

Do you agree that the number one reason someone makes a certain amount of income is an unconscious belief about how much they believe they are worth?

John Assaraf

The Quality of the Relationship with the Self

The quality of life is measured by the quality of relationships. Both of them are determined by the quality of the relationship with the self. Therefore, the recipe for achieving a good quality of life starts by healing the relationship with the self. It involves a three-step process: 1) giving it to oneself (e.g. self-love, self-respect, nurturing); 2) giving it to others; 3) receiving it.

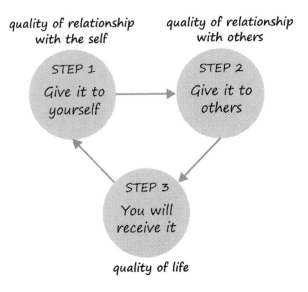

The process is initiated internally by working with the self: when you are able to give yourself self-love and self-respect, then these qualities will automatically reflect in your relationships with others. Their behavior will mirror to you your own consciousness. Love-based internal qualities cause similar qualities to be produced on the external level. The person involved in this process becomes an automatic giver and receiver.

Self-actualization

Moving up the
emotional
frequency scale
(consciousness
translates as
frequency)

⟵ exiting the victimhood
bandwidth

⟵ healing the relationship
with the self
(self-image, self-respect)

⟵ healing low self-worth

⟵ removing emotional blocks

Chapter 4
Emotional Purging

Emotional Purging and Vulnerability: The Nonlinearity of the Healing Process

The healing process is punctuated with ups and downs and is therefore nonlinear. Making a step forward means making half a step back, then another step forward, and so forth. It is like going from one to two, then back to one and a half, then up to two and a half, then back to two. The emotional purging process is an ascending spiral: in order to get from A to B, one must experience the turmoil of one, two, and three (Figure 9). The reason is that as one anchors more and more love-based consciousness, these new frequencies will push to the surface whatever junk is lying at the bottom.

Towards Heroic Probability

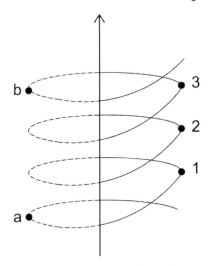

Figure 11. The nonlinearity of the emotional purging process

Things can get bumpy during the surfacing process as one peels the onion layers, revealing hidden stuff that requires attention and healing. Because of this bumpiness, processing the unwanted baggage is delayed by keeping it stored as long as possible in the subconscious mind. Usually, unpleasant life situations and recurrent negative patterns force us to go down to the basement with a flashlight.

Emotional healing can take the form of physical disease. When a heavy emotional pain resurfaces, it can cause a sudden weakness in the immune system. The idea is not to be daunted by the emotional pain as it resurfaces—what we can feel, we can heal. Remaining aware of the many forms that the healing process may take is the best way to expedite the clearing of unwanted baggage.

Surfing Adversity and Emotional Freedom

Miscreation creates karma and manifests as adversity, which is considered to be a learning tool because "what doesn't kill you makes you stronger." We may not agree that adversity is serving a good cause and that we need to experience it in order to grow. Let us not forget that we are in a distorted system of which adversity is a consequence. Hence, there is no need to further praise it as an essential learning tool, no more than religion needs to praise suffering. This perspective is now superseded. Hedonism, despite its flaws—including looking for happiness in all the wrong places—has also proven to be a growth tool, as it is driven by the desire to feel good, through which some spiritual actualization can be achieved.

Ideally, awareness should be cultivated as a tool for accreting consciousness, instead of adversity as a tool to achieve spiritual growth. Lessons don't need to be learned the hard way. However, since adversity is bound to happen, before we can learn to minimize it by replacing miscreation with cocreation, we can indeed learn how to turn an undesirable situation as much as possible into a tool for achieving healing and growth. Adversity is the result of our own and other people's miscreations. Possible constructive ways of handling adversity include using negative situations as mirrors reflecting certain denied aspects of ourselves, or seeing those who caused us emotional pain as Emotional Trainers, as Rhonda Byrne calls them. If the adverse situation is not used constructively to achieve emotional freedom, then it is likely to repeat itself.

Surfing adversity means using a negative situation to achieve emotional freedom in two basic steps: 1) identifying the fear-based program mirrored by the undesirable situation and 2) achieving emotional freedom by shifting to love mode. The first step is about bringing awareness to a particular aspect of the shadow-self, and the second one is about emotional release and transmutation. After step two is successfully completed, cocreation supersedes miscreation and the chances of more adversity coming one's way are minimized. If one has been betrayed by a partner, the emotional pain will likely include feelings of anger, unworthiness, and blame. When such a situation occurs, one can wallow and drown in the emotional pain or decide to outgrow the feelings of anger, unworthiness, and blame by healing the underlying fear-based consciousness that has triggered the negative situation. If one has difficulty completing step one by identifying subconscious programs, working with forgiveness of self and others is an efficient way of achieving a certain degree of emotional release.

Acting Out

Adverse situations can be triggered by the subconscious mind as a way of acting out negative mental and emotional patterns. In psychology, much emphasis is placed on "acting out" as part of the healing process: when negative patterns are not processed internally, the only way for them to be acknowledged and released is through a physical event. Acting out is the scientific version of "walking out the karma," where fear-based programming translates as a negative physical event. Almost every unpleasant event can be perceived as an acting out situation, which it is useful to become aware of in order to do the required emotional processing. The situation of a partner walking out on a relationship can be the acting out of a subconscious fear of abandonment linked to a toxic core belief about one's self-worth, image, and lovability. When progressive mastery of thoughts and emotions is achieved, these painful lessons can be avoided by healing miscreation at its roots, on an energetic level, before it materializes in the physical world.

Chapter 5
Getting in Sync

The Magic of Serendipities

Serendipities are the physical proof that one is in sync with the matrix of creation. In distortion-free dimensions, swift manifestation, or the art of serendipity, is the norm. Difficulties in manifesting occur when one is operating in fear mode. Therefore, limitations and the inability to manifest are the norm on planet earth. The art of swift and synchronized manifestation can be restored through sustained mental and emotional healing. The farther one moves up the healing ladder, the more he will experience the magic of serendipities. The multiplication of positive events and desired outcomes will make life appear magical.

The first tipping point, or the "zero point," beyond which serendipities are likely to start occurring is the 200 Hz threshold on Dr. Hawkins emotional frequency scale, which corresponds to the emotion of courage. It is also the point beyond which exiting the victim/victimizer bandwidth is initiated, as one starts moving from major distortion and blockage toward a minimum level of spiritual health—thus restoring the potential for manifesting desired outcomes and events.

Synchronization with the matrix of creation is achieved by realigning the divine blueprint. Expedited healing requires working on several fronts, namely clearing the shadow-self, and replacing miscreation with cocreation as a daily routine. Experiencing the magic of serendipities is extremely empowering, as one reintegrates his original role as cocreator. Serendipities are signs of spiritual health and synchronicity with the matrix of creation.

Harnessing the Power of Thoughts and Emotions: Restoring the Ability to Manifest

Thoughts and emotions are things; consciousness and intent are forces. In the nonphysical realm, thoughts are instant, whereas in the three-dimensional world there is a variable time lag between an intent and its materialization. This temporal buffer acts as protection; otherwise, if someone got mad at someone else and wished he were dead, this would automatically come true. The time lag between an intent and its manifestation acts like a firewall for those who haven't yet acquired mastery of thoughts and emotions. The materialization of thoughts is not instant in the three-dimensional world mainly because of the high density of matter and the carbon-based nature of the atoms, as well as the presence of fear-based consciousness, which creates conflicting energies that result in a state of cognitive dissonance. If the first cause cannot be remedied, the second one hinges upon free will choice.

Harnessing the power of the mind means working with thoughts and emotions as forces in order to heal existing mental and emotional distortions, monitor and correct present thoughts and emotions, create positive emotional anchor points and open new energy vortices, and move into synchronicity with the matrix of creation—all of which is achieved in the now.

Clearing the distortions of the mental body can be paralleled with consciously redirecting energy and downloading positive mental programs. The immediate rewards of working with thoughts and emotions as forces that shape reality and as tools of realignment with the matrix of creation are the restoration of the ability for swift manifestation, feeling connected to something bigger, and building muscle for controlling one's own reality. Other benefits include evolving beyond the constricted state of consciousness of the victimhood bandwidth, which is equal to a spiritual rebirth.

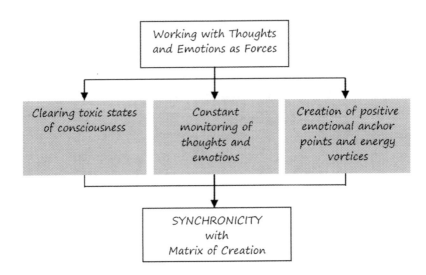

Synchronizing the Mental and Emotional Bodies

Embodying a desired outcome is key to manifestation, and this process requires the mental and emotional bodies to be in a state of synchronization. If you envision yourself as financially successful yet are possessed by the fear of not making ends meet, then your mental and emotional bodies are not in sync—you cannot embody the state of consciousness of a wealthy person. Therefore, the emotional leap separating the two states of consciousness of the present and future selves needs to be made.

The first step consists in envisioning a new paradigm. Once it is embedded in the mental body, the emotional leap can start. The turbulence of the process depends on the load of unwanted baggage and the discrepancy between the emotional frequency levels of the present and future selves. The key to manifestation is aligning the frequency of the present emotional body with that of the future self. If the frequency of the mental vision is not matched by the emotional body, then the desired outcome is unlikely to manifest.

Let us suppose that someone envisions being a successful entrepreneur. If he has self-respect issues, a discrepancy will arise between the present bandwidth and the envisioned one. When the consciousness is split between a present and a future self, the result is a state of cognitive dissonance that blocks manifestation. This discrepancy occurs because the emotional body is still lagging behind. Cognitive dissonance is the result of mentally planting new seeds that contradict the present paradigm and its matching emotional bandwidth. This critical issue can be resolved by raising the emotional frequency level in order to align it with the envisioned paradigm, therefore triggering desired outcomes into manifestation.

Everything is energy, and that's all there is to it. Match the frequency of the reality you want, and you cannot help but get that reality. It can be no other way. This is not philosophy. This is physics.

Albert Einstein

Envisioned bandwidth
(Future Self)

Current bandwidth
(Present Self)

Mental body envisions a future self
and anchors new core beliefs

2

Aligning the present bandwidth
with the envisioned one requires
emotional purging in order to
synchronize the emotional and
mental bodies

Feeling Good is Feeling God: Creating Positive Emotional Anchor Points

Raising one's emotional frequency despite unchanged external situations can be achieved by creating positive emotional anchor points and by training oneself to feel good. How we feel is more important than external events because the subconscious mind cannot tell the difference between an imagined event and a real one. An experiment conducted on two sports teams, where one trained physically while the other trained mentally, resulted in both teams achieving the same results. This trick on the mind is an ingenious tool that can be used to make oneself feel good irrespective of external events. Feeling good will in turn trigger positive life situations that will further reinforce feelings of elation and well-being. This is how a virtuous circle can be initiated.

The role of positive emotional anchor points is to create and maintain a certain level of emotional well-being. These are formed by either recalling happy events or imagining desired states of being and dwelling on their corresponding feelings of elation, harmony, joy, achievement, or tenderness until these positive feelings start forming a reality of their own. Several emotional anchor points corresponding to an array of positive emotions can be created at the same time and recalled in moments of emotional distress. This toolkit helps one stay anchored on positive emotions amid unpleasant external situations. Another benefit of emotional anchor points is that they are energy vortices, or portals, through which events of the same energy signature can be channeled and materialized.

Creating sustainable states of happiness can be achieved mentally, irrespective of external life situations. Shifting to positive emotions is incremental, and when sufficient momentum is built, a beneficial change will start taking place in the physical realm. Because the subconscious mind cannot tell the difference between real and imagined situations, you can train yourself to feel good until emotional well-being becomes a default setting and a virtuous circle is set in motion.

Playing with Mantras

Since mental landscapes are as real as physical ones, and because words create worlds, mantras in the form of customized short statements represent powerful programming tools that are also fun to play with. Playing with personal mantras is a cost-free healing modality where one can come up with customized positive statements related to specific areas that need to be addressed. This process relies on inner guidance with respect to identifying issues and tailoring mantras. It also emphasizes self-sufficiency, as one is singlehandedly creating a healing modality based on his personal needs. When used regularly, mantras have the power to reprogram the subconscious mind. A set of mantras can be repeated for several weeks until one feels that certain aspects of his inner programming have been positively altered, after which they can be replaced by other statements following inner guidance. Mantras can be created to override negative programs and to download new sets of beliefs aligned with the future self.

Examples of personal mantras:

I attract the right people that help me grow in my personal and professional life.

I am a powerful and resourceful creator. I am uniquely talented to achieve all of my goals.

I have an abundance of physical and mental energy. I feel and look great.

John Assaraf

I am worthy of positive relationships in my life.

Natalie Ledwell

Chapter 6
Freedom from the Energetic Harness

How Things Really Work

Putting the pieces of the puzzle together and understanding the true mechanics of life cannot be achieved as long as complementary concepts, such as mind and body or science and spirituality, are perceived as antagonisms. They are meant to work together, just like two sides are needed in order to form a coin, and perceiving them as antagonisms is a major cognitive distortion.

Science is about understanding the mechanics of our physical world; it has revealed through the lens of quantum physics that matter is energy. Energy is another word for consciousness, which is another word for spirit. Hence, science is indirectly trying to uncover the mechanics of spirit and how it creates holograms in the form of physical reality. The dichotomy between science and spirit is artificial since the workings of consciousness and how it steps down to manifest as physical form are all based on scientific paradigms.

When science and spirituality are not working together to unveil the mechanics of creation and cocreation, then linearity imposes its limits, as information is uncovered incrementally through sporadic scientific discoveries. Science did not invent electricity—it only discovered it—but it took humanity thousands of years to tap into this knowledge. If the antagonism between the scientific and spiritual realms is removed, then the intangible structures of consciousness that form the backdrop to our physical world can be more rapidly fathomed. Furthermore, extrasensory perception and transdimensional cognition, instead of being discarded as unscientific, can be used as additional tools for understanding the mechanics of both the spiritual and physical realms and how they interface with each other.

Information is a code that carries an encryption and a frequency. Information that is aligned with the matrix of creation is the code of cocreation carrying the imprint for health, whereas disinformation is a distorted code that has a mutating effect on the divine blueprint. Because the code of cocreation resets the imprint for health, concealing the true mechanics of life and replacing them with a distorted construct of reality is key to the dark agenda; likewise, the intent behind opposing body and mind, science and spirituality, is to institutionalize misinformation, thus embedding a distorted code within the divine blueprint. The inability to put the pieces of the puzzle together equals disempowerment and serves the energetic harness.

Moving Beyond Duality

Understanding that the antagonisms underpinning our construct of reality are actually complementary helps to dissolve a lot of the dualities rooted in misperception. The opposition and imbalance between masculine/ feminine, science/spirituality, and body/mind are cognitive distortions forming a code in misalignment with the matrix of creation. These misperceptions are maintained by a manipulation of the good/bad duality. The imbalance between masculine and feminine upon which religious and social systems are built is legitimized by labeling the values that reinforce it as god-given and the values that are not compliant as wrong or evil. Therefore, moving beyond duality entails mainly understanding the real nature of complementarities disguised as antagonisms and relinquishing judgment, since its role is to maintain in place existing cognitive distortions.

Moving beyond duality is the act of moving beyond judgment, the tool by which the good/bad duality is enforced. Labels such as right and wrong are the by-products of a misused good/bad duality that translates as lovable/ unlovable. The ultimate subconscious desire of being lovable justifies the unwavering compliance of the masses with whatever is labeled as right, thus explaining the transgenerational nature of distorted value systems.

How Cognitive Distortions Feed the Energetic Harness

Fear-based consciousness stored in the shadow-self is the root of cognitive distortions. How do cognitive distortions feed the energetic harness? By conditioning someone to miscreate through an alteration of his perceptual filters that will make him perceive misaligned consciousness as the truth. For example, a parent who confiscates his son's iPod during an entire school year so that he can focus on his studies is perceiving a cruel act as the right thing to do.

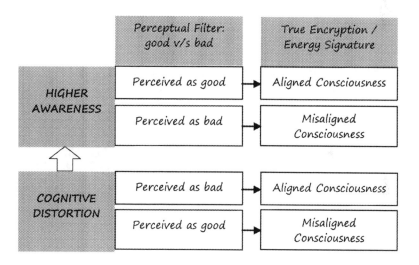

It is not an overstatement to say that everyone suffers to some degree from cognitive distortions. These misperceptions are the root of miscreation, which is the erosion tool of the matrix of creation, producing misaligned consciousness that feeds the parallel matrix. The objective of the energetic harness is to create a transfer of energy from the matrix of creation toward the parallel matrix by transmuting aligned consciousness into misaligned one. This explains the relationship between the shadow-self and cognitive distortions, and how the energetic harness works. Seeding mental viruses with miscreation as a consequence is the primary tool by which the energetic harness operates.

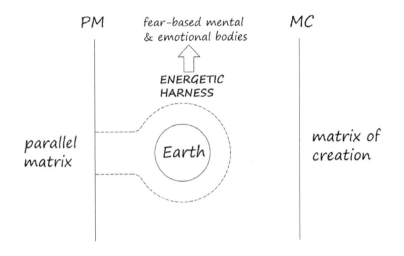

Mechanics of the energetic harness

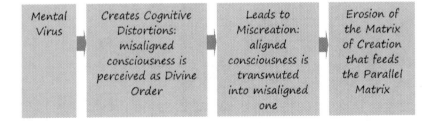

| Mental Virus | Creates Cognitive Distortions: misaligned consciousness is perceived as Divine Order | Leads to Miscreation: aligned consciousness is transmuted into misaligned one | Erosion of the Matrix of Creation that feeds the Parallel Matrix |

Freedom from the Things that Keep Us Energetically Harnessed

The unnatural phenomenon of energetic harnessing can occur if one is stuck along the way during the expansion/contraction cycle. This entrapment takes place if one is in a state of misalignment with the matrix of creation, which means that his divine blueprint has incurred mutations that no longer enable him to engage the contraction cycle. This phenomenon describes the fate of contemporary humanity.

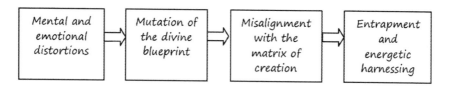

Energetic harnessing is the process through which the quanta of energy that each person represents remains stuck in the lower dimensions, where it can be preyed on by the parallel matrix. Putting an end to quantum draining starts by healing the mental body, which then helps to realign other parts of the intangible anatomy. The distorted reality fields into which our mental and emotional bodies are plugged act as a net, or an energetic harness. By implementing a set of ideas or values that are in misalignment with the matrix of creation under the disguise of official reality or God's will, one is causing distortions in the mental bodies that are plugged into this construct. These translate as mutations and blockages in the divine blueprint with two main results: 1) remaining stuck during the expansion/contraction cycle with reincarnation as a consequence and 2) having one's quanta drained into the parallel matrix, leading to entropy and physical death.

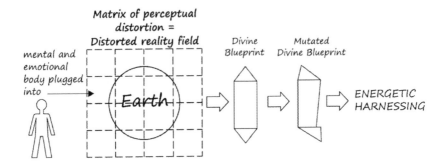

Healing the mind goes beyond manifesting financial wealth and the life of our dreams; it is about spiritual freedom and finding the way back home for those who no longer wish to be trapped inside distorted reality systems. Because it is a tricky endeavor for the mind to discover the true nature of concepts beyond the good/bad label, emotions can be called to the rescue. How emotions can be used as pointers is very simple: whatever makes one contract with unhappiness is unbeneficial, and whatever makes one expand with happiness is. Dwelling on self-depreciating thoughts causes one to contract, which means that what he believes to be true about himself does not serve him and is therefore untrue. Emotions allow us to connect with the energy signature behind the label, which explains why a sense of expansion can be experienced when thinking about something labeled as bad, and vice-versa. Institutionalized concepts that make one feel unhappy or frustrated are distortions—for instance, martyrdom. Learning to navigate through life by filtering what makes one expand allows for a progressive unplugging from the matrix of misperceptions and provides the opportunity to tailor a personalized path more in line with one's spiritual needs.

Snapping Out of the Illusion

When people are clueless about the structure of the universe and their role in it, they are given dogmas and programs to follow. The misaligned nature of these constructs explains the fear-based reality fields that most people manifest. Spiritual maturity that grants freedom from the cognitive distortions of the fear-based matrix entails restoration of the state of knowingness, otherwise known as the divine code.

Snapping out of the illusion is the process of filtering information through the lens of the divine code. A requisite is the will to deconstruct and unlearn canned ideas, namely by relinquishing self-righteousness. The objective is to filter misaligned codes that mutate the divine blueprint, thus feeding the wheel of karma where mental distortions are played endlessly though reincarnation. Snapping out of the illusion simply means no longer being disillusioned by mental constructs that stand in the way of regaining the lost knowingness necessary for spiritual actualization, and for exiting our closed system toward more perfected realms. A new perceptual framework can be incrementally built as one starts extracting himself gradually from the contrived perspective of the official program.

The more information is aligned with the divine blueprint, the higher is its frequency, and the more likely it is to be rejected because of the discrepancy that exists between its frequency level and that of most people. Again, if a radio is tuned to 88 FM, it cannot catch what is being broadcasted on 102 FM. Sometimes the gap can be bridged, which allows for the information not to be rejected—though it is not necessarily accepted. When the gap cannot be bridged, the information is totally discredited. This is the main challenge that keeps most people stuck inside their perceptual illusions.

The Truth about Prince Charming and Other Father Figures

Snapping out of the illusion means deconstructing a wide spectrum of embedded concepts, including Prince Charming, the most popular disempowerment tool for women. Being in a relationship is something to look forward to; however, the way women are brainwashed that they are insignificant until Prince Charming comes along and gives them a respectable status is quite belittling. The consequence of this myth is that women tend to lead passive lives outside from their reproductive role. Prince Charming and other father figures are the donkey's carrot. The path to spiritual actualization cannot be taken if one is waiting to be saved by someone else. It is an individual journey that most of us never take because we choose to be distracted by disempowering myths that we should relinquish our power to Prince Charming and a myriad of other gurus.

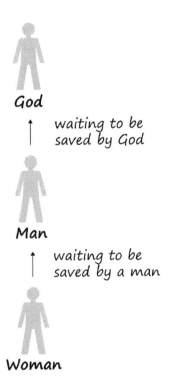

God

↑ waiting to be saved by God

Man

↑ waiting to be saved by a man

Woman

Do Yourself and the World a Favor: Break Free from the Energetic Harness

We cannot be responsible for saving the world, since we did not create it. What we can do instead is be responsible for ourselves. Each person who breaks free from the energetic harness is doing the world a huge favor. When he pulls out his quanta from the harness, he reduces the momentum of the parallel matrix while simultaneously reinforcing the matrix of creation by realigning his consciousness with it. It is about being of service rather than saving the world: one can't do the work or make the choice for others because the healing process is a personal undertaking, but if one is able to maintain a frequency level above the energetic harness, he can be of service to many. There is more chance of touching others positively with restored spiritual health than when one is emotionally and mentally fragmented and harnessed. The process starts with being responsible for oneself and, by doing so, helping others.

Transcending the energetic harness is achieved through mastery of thoughts and emotions. The more emotionally overwhelmed one is feeling, the more energetically harnessed he is. Instead of pushing painful emotions under the rug, one can start by regaining control over his emotional and mental states. Putting an end to emotional overwhelm is like walking one day into a long-forgotten garden and, instead of being daunted by the weeds, making it a habit to return there every day in order to restore balance.

If you want to awaken all of humanity, then awaken all of yourself, if you want to eliminate the suffering in the world, then eliminate all that is dark and negative in yourself.

Truly, the greatest gift you have to give is that of your own self-transformation.

Lao Tzu

Chapter 7
Saving the World from Home

About Worshipping Gods and Following Gurus

In certain Zen teachings, after a person is assigned a guru, he is later told that he never needed one in the first place and that mastery is about becoming one's own guru. The need to worship and to follow—i.e. to receive a set of canned ideas—is so deeply embedded in our mental landscape that the thought of looking for our own answers can seem extremely daunting. Furthermore, the state of disempowerment and passivity that most people indulge in is not conducive to such an undertaking. Because fear-based consciousness pervades our entire system, there is no possibility for a captainship that is exempt from distortion. Spiritual maturity means becoming aware of the status of earth as a raft drifting on the sea of iterative, yet finite, existence with no real captainship. This explains the multitude of religious and philosophical points of views all trying to describe one underlying, mysterious truth. Because every theory needs to be carefully filtered, embracing only one doctrine means accepting as true the distortions it encompasses, in addition to remaining closed to valuable information that is available elsewhere.

Turning On the Internal GPS and Restoring the Connection to Source

The questionability of external captainship is an additional reason to turn inward for guidance. Looking for answers is very much an individual process not achieved by following a mass creed. The internal GPS is a built-in ability that is dormant in most humans, the restoration of which is essential for navigating our physical dimension where fear- and love-based consciousness are closely intertwined. Restoring the connection to Source, and along with it multidimensional awareness, is essential for validating or invalidating information by being able to find out what rings true. Reconnecting with Source also restores the flow of energy that normally exists among a being in biological form, his higher soul, and the matrix of creation, a natural process that counteracts entropy.

Restoring the connection to Source has a three-fold objective: 1) allowing for swift navigation by avoiding distortions and maintaining a state of integrity, 2) being connected to one's true purpose and identity, and 3) restoring the natural flow of energy needed for both spiritual and biological replenishment. A restored connection allows the aligned frequencies to flow in, thus overriding distortions and, most importantly, helping to discover beyond the normalized recipe for life one's unique purpose and contribution.

Working with Personal Guides

No one can win a marathon or graduate from school for us; these are things we need to do for ourselves. The mental landscape that creates our reality is a secret garden that can only be accessed and tended to personally. It is useless to wait for someone to come and save us while we are busy watching TV—everyone needs to do the job for himself. The good news is that we are not alone. Each of us has personal guides that we can work with.

Since our system is full of interference, it is important to establish trust. Communication can take many forms, as one can see his guides with his inner vision, see physical signs, or receive insights from them through direct cognition—i.e., thoughts and ideas. It is important to gain the certainty that one is connected to entities from a love-based dimension. Guides can come from dimensions of pure consciousness beyond embodiment and choose to manifest as an arbitrary form. Connecting with the energy signature is a good way of finding out whether what is being seen or sensed is not deceiving. When holding a vision of a guide that makes itself manifest under a certain form, you can let the emotions flow to you. If it is a deceitful entity, you will feel a sense of uncertainty and eventually unease. If you can't tell right away, you can refrain from interacting with the entity until you receive a clear insight. It takes practice to discern true guidance from ill-intended interference. Once trust has been established, the art of intangible communication can be mastered, and the relationship strengthened, by regularly sending thoughts of gratitude to one's guides.

Saving the World from Home

What if you were told that you can save the world from your living room? Saving the world is not about proselytism and imposing ideas on others. It is much simpler and extremely personal. It comes down to understanding that we are the ones we have been waiting for. Healing personal distortions is the act of saving the world, as one becomes the starting point of an ever-expanding sphere of cocreation. Because the frequency of love-based consciousness overrides anything that is fear-based, every person's sphere of cocreation impacts the environment through morphic resonance and contributes to healing others. When more people undertake transforming their personal universe into a sphere of cocreation, a tipping point will be reached beyond which a collective realignment with the matrix of creation will take place. Saving the world is not about forcing big ideas on others, or even feeding the poor. It is essentially about taking responsibility for one's personal healing and realignment, and fully committing to that.

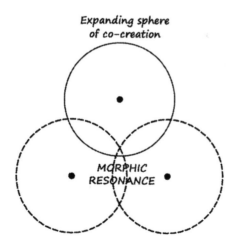

Expanding sphere
of co-creation

MORPHIC
RESONANCE

The Meaning of Cocreation

Every person is the starting point of a circle of creation that has a ripple effect on the environment. The sum of our personal universes is what creates the universe. The meaning of cocreation is more fully comprehended if one is aware of the process through which he creates his personal universe and how this affects his peers and the matrix of creation on a larger scale. The more we grow in awareness, the more we fathom this role. Every second brings with it a dual choice between cocreation and miscreation, whether in thought or in deed. But things are more complicated than they seem, since most people who miscreate are not aware of the real nature and magnitude of their deeds. Unconscious parenting is a good example of that. Before making a choice between cocreation and miscreation, one must be able to tell the difference—especially that miscreation is not only sugarcoated and disguised as the "right thing to do," but it is also institutionalized.

Cocreation requires reaching a state of awareness that enables one to distinguish between an action aligned with the matrix of creation and its opposite. It's a complicated affair because we have no remembrance of a prior, fear-free order. Embodying the role of cocreator, in which every single choice is made in alignment with the matrix of creation, is not compatible with our present mental conditioning and its array of cognitive distortions. The ability to navigate the sea of distorted consciousness and detangle oneself from the universal illusion is a prerequisite for cocreating and recovering the state of godhood that it entails.

The benefits of cocreation on a personal level are a state of permanent expansion, bringing along a limitless field of possibilities. A fear-based state characterized by an attitude of defensiveness, limited possibilities, and a restrained vital space can turn into a state of cocreative expansion, in which one finds himself at the center of an ever-expanding sphere that contributes to the enrichment of the matrix of creation rather than a diseased one that detracts from it.

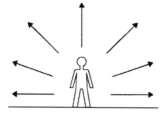

Expanding sphere of co-creation
and limitless possibilities

> 500 Hz

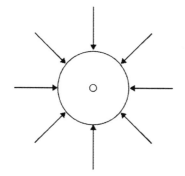

Restrained sphere of miscreation
and countless limitations

< 200 Hz

How do we know that we want to choose cocreation? The answer is simple. We want to avoid miscreation simply because we don't like all forms of suffering and pain, whether emotional, mental, or physical. Miscreation creates a string of abnormalities that nobody enjoys.

The Science of Enrichment

Cocreation is the act of enriching the world. We are more familiar with the science of getting rich than with the science of enrichment. Getting rich is the act of accumulating financial wealth, while enrichment has to do with the accretion of consciousness. They are not contradictory, since the second one is what usually precedes the first.

The science of enrichment is the art of quantum boosting while stopping quantum draining, which is a state of depletion caused by miscreative habits. Because the energy units of a professional football player are all focused on football, he cannot pretend to win the US Open. He needs to disengage himself from football first before refocusing all his energy units on tennis. Similarly, when all our consciousness units are focused on negative habits, we have little energy left to dedicate to quantum boosting. The two-track approach consists of a conscious disengagement of energy units from depleting habits and their redirection toward the fulfillment of a state of mind conducive to the accretion of consciousness.

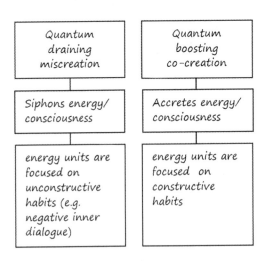

Starting a Virtuous Circle and Random Acts of Kindness

The inner process of healing fear-based consciousness can be further complemented by physical action, namely random acts of kindness that can become, when enough momentum is built, virtuous circles of love-based consciousness. One can start building muscle with random easy to do acts of kindness. The impact of small acts that carry a love-based encryption is extremely powerful. What is important is the energy signature behind the act, rather than the act itself. The more actions with a love-based energy signature are undertaken, the more momentum is built for overriding fear-based morphogenetic fields. A small act of kindness undertaken in Florida could end up affecting the crime rate in New York.

Only a small action is required in order to start a virtuous circle as a stepping stone toward triggering more matching consciousness. It can be something like giving a large tip once a week. After a while of practicing this small action, the desire will be felt to build on it by putting more love-based consciousness in the world. One can choose any small action and start building momentum from there. If everybody decided to initiate a virtuous circle this way, we can only imagine how drastically enhanced our environment would become. All these love-based acts, even if they are sporadic, will end up building a strong morphogenetic field that will override inorganic energies once critical mass is reached.

Chapter 8
Spiritual Actualization

You Are the One You Have Been Waiting For

Spiritual actualization is the process of orchestrating the return to Source. It entails reawakening to the laws of creation and cocreation and to the multidimensional nature of universal structures and personal anatomies. The next step after awareness is restoring the imprint for health to the greatest extent possible. Both steps must be underpinned by the strong intent to return to godhood.

The process of spiritual actualization is about personal awakening, responsibility, and mastery. It requires no middleman, and most importantly it cannot be achieved by waiting passively for a prophet, a messiah, or a hero to come and save us. No one can do for us what we came here to do for ourselves. No one can graduate from school for us. Each one of us is the hero he has been waiting for. Awakening is realizing that we are equal to any prophet or role model because every person is a master in the making. A freshman doesn't look down on a fifth-grade student; they are equal in value, even though one may be more advanced in the learning process. Furthermore, a fifth-grade student is a freshman in the making, and no one can stop him from achieving that except for himself. We are all masters, heroes, and prophets in the making, and no one but ourselves can stand in our way. When we make this realization, it becomes obvious that worship won't get anybody anywhere. If we are stuck, it is because we can't find our way out, and the only exit is through remembering and reclaiming our godhood instead of being a passive victim waiting to be saved by a superhero. It is all about us becoming that superhero. No delegating is allowed; every person's task is to become his own guide and master. If somebody told you to awaken to your inner superhero, why would you say no to godhood?

There Is No One Judging You

The game of life is about spiritual actualization, which means ultimately transcending the human experience. It is not about doing A, B, and C because otherwise we will be punished by God. This perspective characterizes a lack of mental and emotional maturity. It is a major cognitive distortion standing in the way of spiritual growth because it replaces responsibility and proactiveness with passivity and lip service. The game of life is about responsibility to either cocreate or miscreate and awareness of the energetic consequences that each choice represents.

There is no one judging us. Judgment is fear-based and cannot be the attribute of a god that dwells in a love-based dimension. We are taking part in the game of creation and carry with us the consequences of our choices and actions in the form of an energetic imprint. Our fear-based choices will mutate and ultimately destroy our spiritual anatomy, while at the same time eroding the matrix of creation. Hence, we carry our conscious and unconscious choices in the form of an energy signature that determines the landscape of our journey, whether we are in biological or nonbiological form. Responsibility means making conscious love-based choices; this is the path to godhood. It has nothing to do with lip service and Judgment Day.

What Is Spiritual Actualization Anyway?

Spiritual actualization starts by being awake, aware, and able, because getting out of the maze cannot be undertaken in a state of blindness and passivity. It all starts when one is able to catch glimpses of what is beyond the veil and consequently decides to detangle himself from the net of fear and deception.

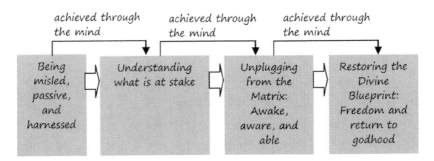

Spiritual actualization is about restoring the imprint for health, which is the process of reawakening the dormant spiritual anatomy. It triggers the nonbiological DNA into activation, thus returning to the mental body its ability to expand its perception beyond the physical realm toward intangible states of consciousness and being.

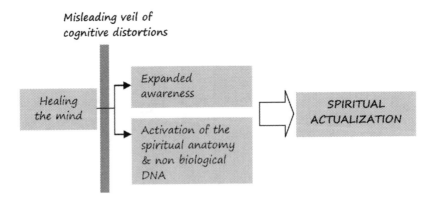

Spiritual actualization is not compatible with universal recipes like the official program because it requires each person to tailor his own path for healing and growth.

Spiritual Integrity and Tough Love

Spiritual integrity and actualization walk hand-in-hand. They both get compromised when a person engages in fear-based behavior or is the recipient of it. A pearl remains a pearl despite being buried under a pile of mud—this describes spiritual integrity. It means not taking part in the distortion and not letting oneself become affected by it.

Exposure to fear-based consciousness is what erodes one's spiritual integrity as he adopts the distorted behavior that is inflicted upon him; from the moment one becomes emotionally engaged, he allows himself to take on the distortion. Maintaining a state of spiritual integrity means not taking part in the distortion mentally, emotionally, or in deed. We should bear in mind that how others act is their karma, how we react is ours.

Tough love is the tool by which spiritual integrity can be maintained. The relationship that Source has with creation is one of tough love, in the sense that anything that threatens the integrity of the matrix of creation gets disconnected. This explains why a mutated consciousness can no longer ascend back to Source and why beseeching does not heal mutated blueprints. Tough love describes the attitude a person adopts when there is an attempt to undermine his self-respect, and erode his spiritual integrity. The idea is not to have a fear-based reaction, but rather to avoid interaction with the victimizer, therefore not allowing for the victim/victimizer distortion to take place. It is important to understand the key role of self-respect in the relationship with the self, others, and Source. Tough love is the legitimate tool that imposes peaceful limits in order to disallow any infringement on the integrity of the soul.

Conscious Mindlessness, Playfulness, and Happiness

Spiritual actualization is not something that is achieved in a Tibetan monastery, and the accretion of consciousness does not exclude conscious mindlessness and playfulness. Working one's way up the emotional scale triggers sustained states of happiness and a desire for conscious playfulness. As fear-based consciousness is transmuted into its opposite and the stifling layers of distortion are gradually peeled off, a sense of one's own innocence gradually emerges. The inner child is no longer afraid to express itself through playfulness and lightness of mind. These are the rewards of emotional freedom that come as a result of healing the mind. Spiritual maturity is freedom from the shoulds, the musts, and the constraints of the official program, and most importantly the burden that comes from thinking that one is not enough and must therefore compete for love. Serious frowns are symptoms of distress rather than a sign of maturity; maturity equals freedom and empowerment, with joy as a consequence. Happiness is what nurtures the soul.

Chapter 9
The Ultimate Purpose: Restoring the Divine Blueprint and Ascension

What Being on Planet Earth Means

Living on planet earth means being part of a mass consciousness that has strayed from its evolutionary path, becoming stuck in a black hole system halfway between the matrix of creation and the parallel matrix. Human consciousness is drifting in these lower dimensions, unaware of what is at stake, busy pursuing carrots on a sinking ship. This three-dimensional drama is rooted in the loss of knowingness and its subsequent replacement with misaligned paradigms. Cocreation requires a certain level of awareness, in the absence of which miscreation prevails with its detrimental consequences on the divine blueprint.

The true nature of information is that of a code from which a certain reality is birthed. The orchestrated loss of the divine code and its purposeful replacement with distorted paradigms has generated irregularities that were not part of the original plan, including fear, pain, suffering, karma, aging, death, reincarnation, the formation of the shadow-self and negative ego, and the loss of abilities, namely manifestation and ascension. The evidence that things are not as they should be is overwhelming in our daily lives. This may sound dramatic, but despite the fact that awakenings are sometimes harsh, they are worth every effort because they carry the promise of awareness and the limitless power that comes along with it. It is worth pushing that door open, even if it means having to walk down a dark, scary hallway. The only way to get to the other side is by making the effort to cross.

Restoring the Divine Blueprint

The romantic myth of going to heaven is really about restoring our original settings. Realigning the divine blueprint requires genuine healing and cannot be achieved through lip service. It is the process of restoring the different components of the secret anatomy to their original settings, thus enabling ascension to distortion-free realms. Ascension is part of the contraction cycle that follows every expansion cycle, which consists of consciousness expanding from Source in order to express itself through cocreation. When miscreation takes place, the return cycle to Source is either hindered or completely blocked. Because of the current state of misalignment of our biological and spiritual anatomies, the reality we have been experiencing, regardless of whether we are embodied or not, is comparable to a "Groundhog Day."

Most people do not find our distorted reality construct flawed and will therefore choose to endorse it. They will filter and reject any information that offers a different perspective. Others who have a different longing may choose to venture on the road less traveled. Healing and restoring the divine blueprint will then appear as the primary purpose in life. It involves mainly replacing distorted codes with the divine code by restoring the true knowingness related to the mechanics of creation and multidimensional existence.

Restoring the imprint for health involves activating dormant DNA strands with the possibility of achieving a twelve-strand activation and beyond. Each DNA strand can be compared to a music note. Operating with only a few active strands, like most people do, is very limiting—what possibilities do "Re" and "Do" offer? Conversely, operating with twelve activated strands is like having twelve music notes with limitless possibilities of musical expression.

Critical Mass and Morphic Resonance

Since everything is connected and love-based consciousness has the power to override distortions, each person who engages in the healing process initiates a positive shift with a rippling effect on the environment. According to Dr. Hawkins, one person who calibrates at 700 Hz on the emotional frequency scale can make up for hundreds of thousands of people calibrating below 200 Hz. Furthermore, if a critical mass of individuals engaged in the healing process is reached, then a collective quantum shift will take place as a result of the code being altered at the level of the morphogenetic field. Those who consciously choose to take the path of the return to godhood are concomitantly paving the way for others, even if they seem to be engaged in this process on a personal level. This illustrates the pertinence of Gandhi's statement about the wish to change the world being the act of changing oneself. It also demonstrates how powerful and important every single person is. If one makes the decision to have a huge impact on the world and commits to it, so he shall. It is really about becoming who we already are, an emanation of God that has ventured to the confines of the universe. Socrates' "become who you are" is an invitation to go back home.

Your Life, Your Rules

We spend our lives running away from emptiness, for which desire is the usual antidote. The satisfaction of a desire like buying the car of our dreams has the virtue of temporarily filling that void. But where does this feeling that everyone experiences come from? Let us remember that emotions are pointers, including negative ones like the feeling of emptiness. They are the instrument that the higher soul uses to communicate with its incarnated counterpart. The feeling of emptiness simply means that there is a destination for us that we haven't yet reached, and that we are walking in the wrong direction. It is drawing our attention to what is really at stake, including the fact that there is something wrong with our anatomy and the dimension that we are evolving in when we are too busy channeling our energy toward the fulfillment of mundane commitments.

Listening to the voice of the soul entails facing the feeling of emptiness instead of spending tremendous efforts trying to run away from it. What if that disagreeable feeling was actually trying to tell us something? When we find ourselves in a situation or a relationship that is no longer serving us, the pain that we experience is like a friend nudging us to make the necessary changes. The disagreeable feeling of emptiness is nudging us to live a substantial life, rather than a shallow one dictated by pre-established rules, and to fathom what is really at stake when we are too caught up in the game of survival. Its primary message is to stop wasting energy decorating a sinking ship. It is telling us to simply get off that ship.

From that perspective, the antidote to shallow living and mere survival is to tune into the voice of the soul, which leads to a more personalized path as one becomes the cocreator of his own rules. Each person needs to tailor his own path in order to do the necessary realignment of the divine blueprint required for exiting our closed system and to achieve spiritual actualization, which is the role that each person is meant to play in the cocreation game. Each healing path is different; therefore, spiritual actualization means cocreating one's own rules. The more we are able to achieve that for ourselves, the more we will experience a heightened sense of being and the further we will be able to go on our journey back to Source.

How Far Will You Go?

Should you decide that you wish to realign your consciousness with the matrix of creation in order to pursue your journey back to Source, you need to understand a simple fact: organic light is our fuel, and the more of it we hold, the farther we will go. Organic light is love-based consciousness, or the divine code. Each person has a certain percentage of organic and inorganic light. Restoring the imprint for health is the process of healing fear-based consciousness, which is the act of transmuting inorganic into organic light.

A person with an expanded awareness and a desire to return to innocence understands why restoring the imprint for health is the primary purpose of life. Destiny is not a matter of chance; it is a matter of choice. It is not something that we wait for, but something that we accomplish.

Part IV

Back to Godhood in a Few Steps

Chapter 1
Three Steps to Mastery and Godhood

Toward Godhood: Envisioning and Actualizing the Future Self and Heroic Probability

What does godhood mean, anyway, and how does it relate to each one of us? Godhood can be defined as a state of constant cocreation, accompanied by a permanent state of feeling good. Feeling good is feeling god, so what makes you happy? Each one of us is capable of envisioning a future self that represents the best of who we can become in this lifetime. The future self is not exempt from distortions, since it is envisioned by a mentally and emotionally immature consciousness. It will become more aligned with the heroic probability as one becomes more spiritually mature. Actualizing this future self, or heroic probability, is the closest we can get to godhood in this lifetime.

In mainstream culture, the pursuit of godhood involves giving up desire and retiring from the world to some remote monastery. What if it were much simpler than that? Godhood is about achieving a constant state of cocreation and can therefore be undertaken from our own living room. When all of a person's thoughts, emotions, deeds, and frequencies that he is emitting are love-based, he will know he is there. It surely doesn't mean that we need to give up desire along with the things that make us happy. Happiness is more guaranteed to bring us closer to godhood than frustration. The more we grow into awareness, the more our desires will become spiritually mature and oriented toward the accretion of consciousness and frequency.

The roadmap for getting there includes two important milestones that correspond to the two thresholds of 200 Hz and 500 Hz on the emotional frequency scale. These thresholds determine three bandwidths, or energy signatures, that translate as different reality fields.

Bandwidth 1 is the victimhood bandwidth, where the energetic harness is very strong.

Bandwidth 2 is where the process of self-actualization can start.

Bandwidth 3 is where freedom from the energetic harness is achieved, and with it the potential for ascension.

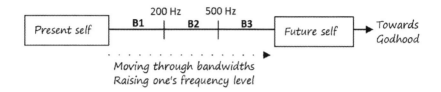

Moving from the present self toward the future one means moving through bandwidths by raising one's frequency level. Inorganic fear-based consciousness is what lowers our frequency, and raising it again is achieved by transmuting fear-based consciousness into love. The fear-based consciousness that we can easily identify and work with is comprised in the mental and emotional bodies. Identifying negative thoughts and emotions and replacing them with positive ones initiates the healing of other inorganic components of the divine blueprint.

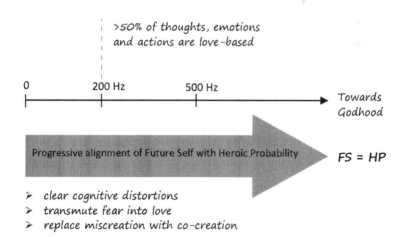

Other methods aimed at restoring the divine blueprint, like reactivating the DNA or the merkaba, will not be tackled. These mechanics are very complex, and their misuse can have dramatic consequences, such as provoking a state of reversal mode.

Three Steps to Mastery and Godhood

To each of the three main bandwidths corresponds an energy signature that translates as a physical reality field. Moving from the lower bandwidths, where most individuals are likely to be stuck, toward the higher ones can be done in three major steps:

Step 1 – Exiting the Victim/Victimizer Bandwidth

Step 2 – Self-Actualization: Your Life, Your Rules

Step 3 – Freedom from the Energetic Harness and Ascension: Yes, Your Life Is Absolutely Magical

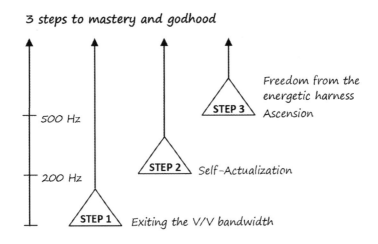

Each step hinges upon the previous one, since the process of self-actualization cannot start if one is still operating in victimhood mode. Likewise, ascension, which is exiting our closed system, cannot take place if one hasn't freed himself from the energetic harness.

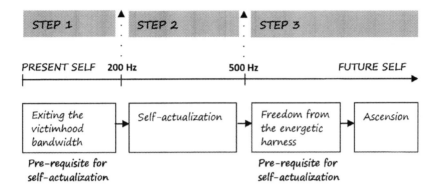

The energy signature that corresponds to the victimhood bandwidth is burdened with a high percentage of inorganic light along with significant mental and emotional distortions. This bandwidth is comparable to a spiritual grave, in the sense that nothing can be achieved when one is operating in such a low frequency mode. To stop operating in victimhood mode, whether as a victim or as a victimizer, is an absolute prerequisite for exiting the "hamster on a wheel" bandwidth. Unfortunately, this distortion is widespread, and its morphogenetic field is a powerful matrix in which most individuals are entangled. It acts as a powerful energetic harness draining energy from those who are ensnared in it, thus justifying vampirism as the primary survival tool in this reality field. Empowerment and self-actualization can only start when one is out of the victim/victimizer bandwidth.

Once out of the victimhood and vampirism bandwidth, one is empowered enough to start incrementally paving a more personalized path in line with his own spiritual needs. Self-actualization starts as one cocreates his own rules and is no longer enslaved by the obligation of remaining confined to a preconceived role. When this process starts, it means that the person is now well advanced in the healing process of the shadow-self, which involves the clearing of mental and emotional distortions and leads to a progressive freedom from the matrix of fear-based consciousness. Freedom from the energetic harness is achieved not only by healing the shadow-self, but also by freeing oneself from fear-based concepts disguised as the sacred. If one is still ensnared in these institutionalized distortions, then he is not free from the energetic harness.

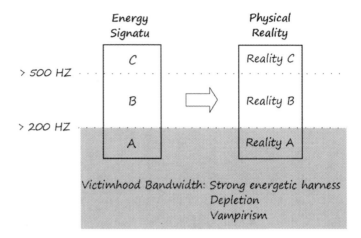

Step 1 – Exiting the Victim/Victimizer Bandwidth

The victim/victimizer bandwidth has the following characteristics:
- Victim or victimizer role
- Strong shadow-self dominating the personality, with significant mental and emotional distortions (e.g. low self-worth)
- Strong cognitive distortions and an inability to filter what is aligned and sacred from what is unsacred and misaligned; fear-based consciousness is mistaken for divine order
- High percentage of inorganic light, and thus distortions in the DB and misalignment with the MC
- Strong energetic harness
- Vampirism, depletion, and the need to drain energy from the environment

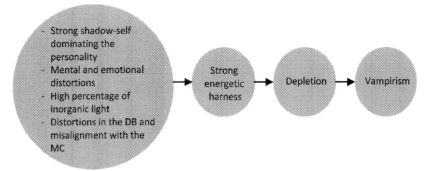

The most painful part of being in this bandwidth is probably the lack of control that one has over his reality field. People experience life as happening to them. The choices they make are unenlightened and do not serve them. They are dictated by cognitive distortions by which the unsacred is perceived as sacred. When most choices are dictated by the matrix of fear-based misperception, the energetic harness has a stronghold on the individual. The consequence is a constant state of misalignment and depletion, and thus vampirism. This form of violence can be directed toward others, but also toward the self, which explains the self-destructive behavior that many people are engaged in.

Exiting the victim/victimizer bandwidth starts by clearing the first layer of shackles, the shadow-self and karma, and allowing for a progressive healing of the relationship with the self. Self-respect and self-image are the pillars of self-actualization; they can be restored by healing the relationship with the self, the quality of which depends on the load of fear-based baggage that one is carrying.

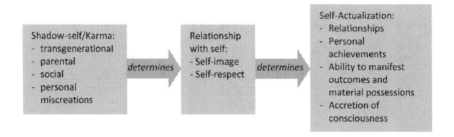

Although the healing modalities of the shadow-self may differ, the only way to get there is by replacing fear-based consciousness with love and miscreation with cocreation. The major roadblock is the veil of misperception, or cognitive distortions that cause one to make unenlightened choices.

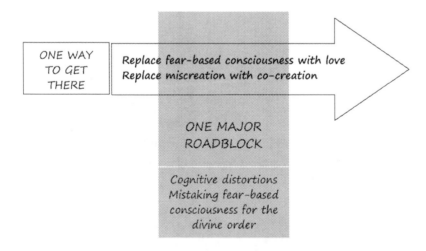

Tuning into the inner guide and listening to oneself is the best way to deconstruct the veil of misperception. What makes you happy? What makes you expand? In this process, you are your own guru as you gradually extract yourself from the mold and incrementally give birth to yourself. As Erich Fromm says, "Man's main task in life is to give birth to himself."

Step 2 — Self-Actualization: Your Life, Your Rules

As you commit to actualizing your future self and heroic probability, you will incrementally raise your frequency level and pull yourself out of victimhood. Mastery of thoughts and emotions begins outside of the victim/victimizer bandwidth when more than half of your thoughts, emotions, and actions become love-based. As you learn to direct energies in a cocreative way, not only do you become the architect of your life, but you also turn into a vortex of love-based consciousness, raising the frequency of the environment.

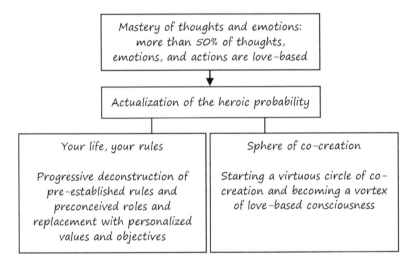

When mastery replaces victimhood, it grants the ability to deconstruct pre-established rules and preconceived roles that are not serving a person to his highest purpose. It replaces them with more personal values and objectives in line with the envisioned future self. Actualizing the heroic probability becomes more important than complying with the official program. Hence, the core value of the victim/victimizer bandwidth, which is complying with the official program by following pre-established rules and preconceived roles, is replaced by a new core value—the actualization of the heroic probability.

These are the main characteristics of the self-actualization bandwidth:
- Replacing victimhood with mastery
- Actualizing the heroic probability instead of complying with the official program
- Becoming a vortex of love-based consciousness and raising the frequency of the environment

Starting a virtuous circle of cocreation is the first step toward godhood. Instead of being a black hole vortex that drains energy from the environment, one becomes a responsible white hole vortex supplying the environment with love-based consciousness. This is the point where life becomes magical.

V/V Bandwidth	Self-actualization Bandwidth
✓ Core Value: Compliance with the Official Program ✓ Victimhood ✓ < 50% of thoughts, emotions and actions are love-based ✓ Pre-established rules and preconceived roles (Official Program) ✓ Vampirism, black hole vortex, drains energy from the environment ✓ Passivity and miscreation ✓ Stronghold of the energetic harness	✓ Core Value: Actualizing the Heroic Probability ✓ Mastery ✓ > 50% of thoughts, emotions and actions are love-based ✓ Personalized values and objectives in line with heroic probability ✓ Love-based vortex, puts energy into the environment ✓ Sphere of co-creation (first step towards godhood) ✓ Progressive freedom from the energetic harness

Step 3 — Freedom from the Energetic Harness: Yes, Your Life Is Absolutely Magical

Once we commit to starting and expanding our sphere of cocreation, the process of transmutation of fear to love, and inorganic light to organic light has been set on automatic pilot. This will gradually restore the imprint for health by clearing the distortions of the divine blueprint and realigning it with the matrix of creation. When you are able to achieve that for yourself, you have mastered the rules of cocreation and the art of serendipities and are now the architect of your life. Not only will you be able to heal your personal hologram, but you will also heal others by being a vortex of love-based consciousness. But the ultimate power that reclaiming one's godhood grants is freedom from the energetic harness, along with the restoration of one's ability to ascend back to distortion-free realms. What this truly means is that each one of us is the prophet he has been waiting for.

The worst form of disinformation is making people believe they will be saved by personas, statues, and icons. It is equal to a spiritual assassination. When we realize that each one of us is the one he has been waiting for, and that the power to break free from the energetic harness lies within, life becomes absolutely magical. It is our construct of reality that is depriving us from that magic. Freedom starts in the mind from the present moment, which means right now.

Chapter 2
The Toolkit for Becoming God

Actualizing the Heroic Probability: The Toolkit for Becoming God

Actualizing the heroic probability is the act of operating an integral shift to love mode through cocreation. The objective is to achieve an integral state of mental, emotional, and physical cocreation that corresponds to the heroic probability, with whom your future self should be aligned if you have reached spiritual maturity. The toolkit for becoming god includes the actualization of the heroic probability as the goal, the emotional frequency scale as the roadmap or reference scale, and a set of tools that includes the mind, the emotional body, and the present moment. These operational tools will allow you to raise your frequency level and move through bandwidths. Not only does the mind play a key role in directing energies and transmuting fear into love, but also this control center can only be accessed in the present moment. The role of emotion is to act as a compass, helping the mind find its way out of the maze of misperceptions by connecting with the energy signature behind ideas and precepts. Therefore, regardless of the healing modalities that one may choose, the mind and the now, in addition to the emotional body, remain key tools.

In addition to this toolkit, each person can choose the appropriate techniques and healing modalities to expedite mental and emotional healing. There may be a limit to what can be achieved in this present lifetime. Reaching that limit represents the first stepping stone on the journey back to heaven, or the flawless state of feeling good.

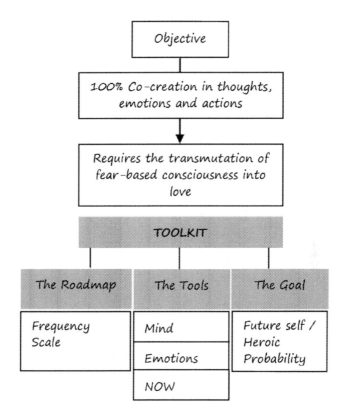

The Three-Step Process of Actualizing the Future Self

Because the heroic probability may seem too daunting, it is easier to start by actualizing the future or ideal self. When a person's frequency level is too low, thinking about achieving the heroic probability will cause him to contract, and since we are emotional beings, this feeling of unease will make him turn away from such a difficult goal. Thinking about the future self, which is the ideal self, is more likely to make us expand with hope and happiness. We can therefore pursue the actualization of the future self as a stepping-stone toward the heroic probability and godhood—despite the fact that this mental construction may not be exempt from distortions, depending on how mentally and emotionally mature each person is.

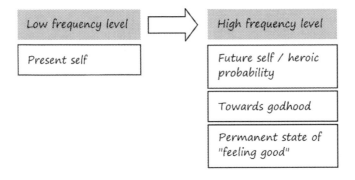

Just like the present self has mental, emotional, and physical characteristics, so does the future self. When we envision our future selves, what we are mainly interested in are the physical characteristics or life situation of the ideal self, the materialization of which involves a three-step process. First, the correct mental programs that support the future self must be embedded in the mind. Then, in the second step, the emotional body needs to be synchronized with the mind. When the right programs are embedded in the mind and the emotional body has anchored the frequency that matches these programs, desired outcomes materialize as a third and final step.

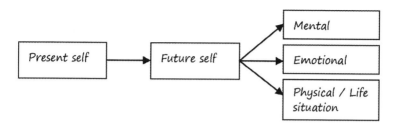

The first step consists of embedding the correct mental programs that form the code of the future self. This is achieved by clearing toxic beliefs that act as roadblocks while simultaneously downloading positive programs that support the vision that one holds of his future self. Then comes an absolute requisite, which is synchronizing the mental and emotional bodies. Once core beliefs about the future self are embedded in the mind, the frequency of the emotional body must be aligned with that of the mental body.

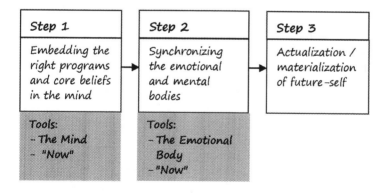

To achieve your goals, you must emotionalize your future self in the present moment so it becomes as real or more real than your current reality.

John Assaraf

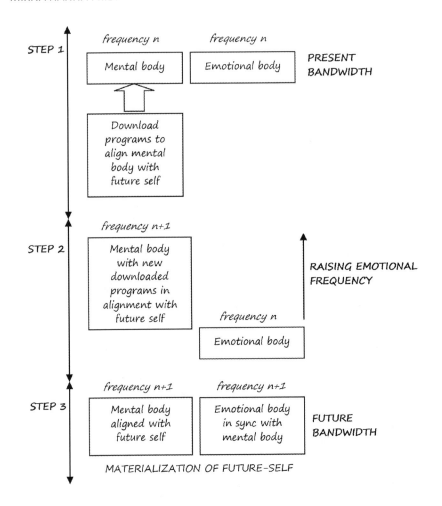

Conclusion

Understanding Oneness

Understanding oneness comes with the awareness of personal and universal multidimensional structures. As seen in the stepping-down process, our spiritual anatomy is multidimensional, and part of it dwells in love-based dimensions located beyond duality. Expanding one's consciousness to these higher realms can help anchor progressively love-based frequencies in the lower dimensions. When one knows he is an expanded being rather than a finite one confined to a physical body, and that part of his anatomy dwells in dimensions beyond fear, he can no longer remain engaged in the victim/victimizer game. The awareness of dwelling simultaneously in a dimension free from miscreation entails that, on some level, one already is and has what he longs for. This expanded consciousness allows for the embodiment of positive states of being: the fastest way to "become", is to remember that on some level one already "is."

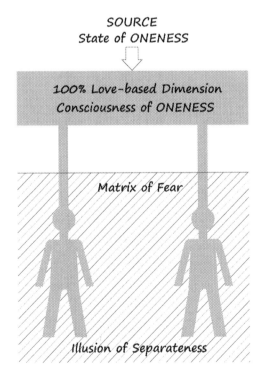

SOURCE
State of ONENESS

100% Love-based Dimension
Consciousness of ONENESS

Matrix of Fear

Illusion of Separateness

Becoming aware of multidimensional structures is key to understanding the initial state of oneness of all there is. The main illusion maintained by fear is the illusion of separateness that feeds the victim/victimizer game, the rat race, political agendas, and our daily routines filled with competition. Awareness of the initial state of oneness will positively alter our emotional response to fear-based stimuli. Shifting our consciousness to the love-based dimensions from which we originate is a powerful tool for eroding the fear-based matrix. Because we originate from a love-based dimension, all fear-based consciousness is alien to us and therefore very alienating.

Hijacking the Universal Mechanics of Cocreation

The mechanics of creation that dictate how consciousness steps down from Source into manifestation are universal. This knowledge was once part of human consciousness, until a series of abnormalities took place. We are now condemned to be born and to live our lives in a state of amnesia, unaware of our multidimensional anatomy. The disabling of the human anatomy is mainly a result of the deactivation of the original twelve strands of DNA, in addition to the misalignment of the mental body by implementing mind viruses that create cognitive distortions and impede us from grasping the universal truth.

Religion, science, New Age, philosophy, and even social constructs are trying to capture parts of this lost knowingness; they are pervaded with distortion because they all legitimize to some extent fear-based consciousness disguised as the "right" values and God's will. They end up forming a convex mirror that only reflects back deformed images. Hence, the official paradigm as a syncretism of religion, science, New Age, philosophy, social constructs, etc., is a deformed reflection of the universal mechanics of creation. Its by-product, the official program, is another fake construct that acts as the normalized recipe for life.

The universal mechanics of creation, or divine order, are cloaked in a veil of cognitive distortion impeding the mind from decoding the truth. The mind remains locked, along with the incarnated soul, in the holographic illusion of three-dimensional reality. The way out of the cloak of misperception is through the mind. It is the tool by which cognitive distortions are corrected and the official paradigm deconstructed.

What fantasy have I made more real than the awareness that would create a different reality?

Dr. Dain Heer

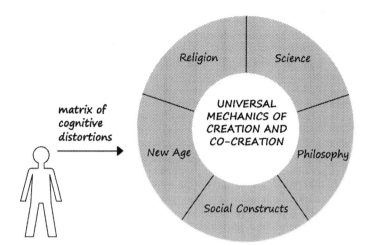

Opening Windows through the Mind

The mind can either close or open windows, depending on how it is used. It is presently conditioned to perceptual confinement by rejecting and labeling as elucubration information that does not pertain to the prevailing scientific or religious paradigms. Imagine living in a room and thinking that that space with the people in it are all there is, when in reality there is a whole world out there. We are more than we think, regardless of the limitations that we might be experiencing, and things may not be as they seem to be or as we have been told. It is always useful to question things, especially if they don't serve us. Opening windows through the wall of misperception requires a mental deconstruction of the prevailing paradigm.

The fact that everything is cloaked in misperception may seem alarming, but it is important not to be overtaken by the drama. Giving in to fear-based thoughts and emotions would represent a misuse of this information. The aim here is to provide a pedagogic compilation of essential tools that are unfortunately not yet part of mainstream culture, thus creating a stepping-stone toward a broader awareness and a heightened sense of being.

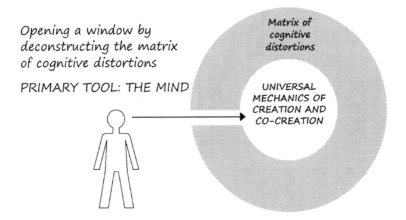

Opening a window by
deconstructing the matrix
of cognitive distortions

PRIMARY TOOL: THE MIND

Matrix of
cognitive
distortions

UNIVERSAL
MECHANICS OF
CREATION AND
CO-CREATION

It is never too late to awaken to the fact that official reality, labeled as "the norm," is the product of a series of interwoven misperceptions. No, we are not alone in the universe, the purpose of life is not the official program, and we did not evolve from monkeys. Instead, we became ones. We are a mutated race trapped in a closed system subject to entropy that needs to be exited. Each individual, as a cell in the big body of humanity, plays a crucial role in the healing process, which gets set on automatic pilot once a critical mass of healed individuals is reached.

Are things really as simple as that? Yes, they are.

About the Author

Mirna Hanna is an architect and urban planner who also holds an MBA, a master's degree in wealth management, and a PhD in urban planning from the Sorbonne. Before becoming interested in self-help and spirituality, she published two poetry books in France. Her book *Is God Evil?* is the result of more than a decade of research in the fields of psychology, self-empowerment, alternative healing techniques and modalities, New Age philosophy, and spirituality.

www.mirnahanna.com